THE WAY

Biblical Truths Revealed

Michelle Webster

ISBN 979-8-89112-877-4 (Paperback)
ISBN 979-8-89112-878-1 (Digital)

Covenant Books
11661 Hwy 707
Murrells Inlet, SC 29576
www.covenantbooks.com

Dedication

I DEDICATE THIS BOOK to my sister, Danielle, who has always inspired me to dream big and to pursue what I love. She has taught me to work hard and to aspire to be more and use my talents and gifts to follow my dreams. I love God, and pursuing him and his kingdom brings true happiness to my soul. Pursuing his will and calling for my life has helped me discover my true identity and worth. Thank you, Danielle, for inspiring me to get out of my comfort zone and try something new. I am grateful for your leadership in this area of my life. I continue to pray for God to bless you with his goodness and protection all the days of your life.

Preface

I FEEL GOD HAS called me to write this book, and so I want to begin by praying: "Father God, I ask that you guide me and lead me in this journey I feel you have called me on. I pray that you write this book for me through your Holy Spirit within me. I pray that the words chosen are your words and your truth, not my own. I pray that every word written is yours and accomplishes only your will for your kingdom, your power, and your glory. I pray this in the powerful name of Jesus Christ. Amen."

I am committing to praying this each time I walk away from this book and return to it. May God guide this journey and use it for his good purposes.

My Purpose

I AM PASSIONATE ABOUT the Word of God, and anyone who knows me knows that I love Jesus. I truly want nothing more than for everyone on this planet to know Jesus and the love and power of the God we serve. Our God is infinite, all-knowing, all-loving, and all-powerful. Nothing is too big or too impossible for our God. I say this from firsthand experience. God has been moving powerfully in my life since the beginning. As I continue growing in faith day by day, I have become more fully aware of my great need for Jesus to be a CONSTANT part of my life. Only when I began to seek making my relationship with God the strongest relationship in my life did I fully see how BIG he was. When I aligned my life with his will and first sought to be fulfilled in life by him not by material things or people around me, then I was able to fully see the glory and greatness that is our God!

I have seen countless prayers answered. I have felt peace when there was chaos all around me. I have seen God move mountains to protect me and the ones I love. I have seen God make a way in my life when it felt and looked like there was no way. I have been blessed beyond measure, and my God gives to me generously when I ask him for things. This is because I am his precious daughter. He created me, he knows me, and he loves me. I spend time with him daily, and I abide in him. I look to him for love, comfort, strength, wisdom, guidance, help, and peace. I do not search this world for answers but ask my Father who knows all and created all. I abide in him and love him first. Because of that, I am able to receive his great love for me and extend that love to those around me. Unfortunately, I do not do this perfectly by any means. I am a work in progress and a sinner just like everyone else. The difference is I KNOW I need a savior because I cannot be holy or blameless on my own. It is only through the blood of Jesus Christ that I have been made clean and right with God. I recognize that and I thank Jesus daily for that gift. God no longer sees me as a sinner but as his precious child through the lens of Jesus Christ who has washed me clean.

I try every day to model the love of Jesus to those around me. Some days, I kill it and do great work for his kingdom, but many days, I fail and need his grace and forgiveness, which he gladly gives to me. Then I try again the next day to do better. As long as he gives me a tomorrow, I will try hard to serve him with the time I am given. And when I fail and stumble—which he already knows I will but he loves me anyway—I will call on his strength to get up, brush off the dust, and try again. That's all he requires of me, and in return he promises me a beautiful life here on earth where he is always with me and available to me for whatever I need. More importantly, he promises me eternal life with him in paradise when my time on this earth is over.

God's favor and promises are not only for me. This relationship that I enjoy with God is available to all those that seek it. Living a life any other way is a life wasted. God has so much goodness to show you. If you feel like anything in your life is missing, that's because it is! If God is not the center of your life and your number one priority, your life is out of order, and you will never know true peace or happiness. If anyone's opinion of you is more important than the creator of all things, you will never measure up, and you'll always feel "not good enough." If anything in your life is more important to you or a higher priority than God is, your life will never feel whole. You'll always be searching for more.

People spend their whole lives looking for the next thing to fulfill them: the perfect spouse, the perfect job, a child, a promotion, more prestige, more credentials, a better title, a new house, a new car, fame, fortune, acceptance from others, etc.—the list goes on. As many of you know, those things, once achieved, never bring true happiness and rarely fill that void, even for just a moment. Your soul still searches for something else because what you're searching for is not from this world, so the void can't be filled by people or things of this world. If you look to anything other than God for fulfillment in life, you will never know true happiness. You will always feel a sense of something missing no matter what earthly status you climb to. God designed us to long for him. He wants us to search for him and know him. He promises if we seek him, we will find him. He designed us with a hole in our hearts and lives that only he can fill. Once you decide to put him in the center of your life, the hole closes forever, and you are a new creation. It is an amazing, powerful feeling that can only be experienced, not described or explained.

I want to help guide as many people as I can in whatever time I have left on this earth to the key to truth, love, and happiness. The truth of God and his Son Jesus and the truth of the Bible. I want to live out my purpose by pointing others to a living God that saves. I want to invite everyone to experience the love and freedom that I experience. My purpose for this book is to show more people the love and peace that I have found in life from following Christ and reading Scripture. A lifetime of blessing and protection and love is available to everyone. The Word of God is our manual on how to live our lives. It tells us who God is and who God created us to be. The Word of God is truly life-giving and life-changing. It is a beautiful story of God's love and his promises to all those who accept his love and love him back. I want to help point others to truth and to Jesus.

I invite you all to receive the glorious gifts God has for you and the beauty of what he wants to do in you and through you. A walk with God is a lifelong journey, and only time will deepen it further. I am still seeking and still learning and always will be. God regularly gives me more wisdom and understanding of his kingdom when I spend time reading the Bible and abiding in him. God does not reveal all his glory to humans fully or at one time. Over more than a decade, I feel like God has been showing me his heart and his vision for this world and the next. I want to help speed along the process for others by trying to help sum up, using the Word of God, what has taken me decades to discover. I want to help open up Scripture to people in a new way as I feel God has done for me. I want to simplify the complex subject of God in a way that will draw people to seek him and leave them hungry to know him more. I want to fill you all with the promises, hope, and blessings that Scripture gives us. I hope to show you all how vital reading your Bible is to growing your relationship with God. I want to save you all the time and the heartache I spent trying to do this life without God at the center. I want to point you all to truth and peace in knowing Jesus through the written words of Scripture. I pray for each and every person reading this book to have God open your heart and mind to whatever it is he has for you through his written words, not my own. In Jesus's name, amen!

Who Is God?

I S THERE A GOD, and if so, who is he? These are the two biggest and most important questions mankind has ever pondered. This topic has been widely debated since the beginning of time. God is a hard concept to grasp for us humans. This is because God is not of this world, and he doesn't fit into our man-made concepts. We simply have no terminology or concepts that would accurately describe the greatness that is God. To try and understand who God is, we must rely on what God tells us he is. God simply tells us, *"I am who I am" (Exod. 3:14)*. Although this concept is easy for God, it leaves us humans confused and searching for more. We try to make God fit into our constraints of time and space and other human factors, but God cannot and will not fit there. God says, *"I am the alpha and the omega, the first and the last, the beginning and the end" (Rev. 22:13)*. The Bible starts by saying, *"In the beginning GOD CREATED the heavens and the earth" (Gen. 1:1; emphasis mine)*. I hope you caught that God was already there in the beginning. He is the beginning. God was not CREATED; he is the CREATOR. He always was and always will be.

I know this concept is crazy and hard to grasp. I admit I have a lot of questions about all this myself; I can't wait to ask him all my questions one day in heaven. Until he clears it all up for me one day, my faith will have to be sufficient. Faith is the belief or complete trust and confidence in what is unseen and the belief in the promises to come. *"Now faith is the assurance of things hoped for, the conviction of things not seen" (Heb. 11:1)*. Faith can be really hard for some people; many people feel they must see something to believe in it. But Scripture tells us that we are blessed when we believe on faith alone. Jesus said, *"Blessed are those who have not seen yet have believed" (John 20:29).* God is our Creator, and God is our Father. God is the father of all humankind and the creator of all things. God made all things and is in all things. All good things are from God.

"The God who made the world and everything in it is the Lord of heaven and earth and does not live in temples built by human hands and is not served by human hands, as if he needs anything. Rather, he himself gives EVERYONE life and breath and EVERYTHING else. From one man he made all nations, that they should inhabit the whole Earth; and he marked out their appointed times in history and the boundaries of their lands. God did this so that they would seek him and perhaps reach out for him, though he is not far from any of us. For in him we live and move and have our being. As some of your own poets have said 'We are his children'" (Acts 17:24–28; emphasis mine).

We are all children of the same God. This makes us, humans, all brothers and sisters. It doesn't matter where you were born or when or what race, nationality or religion you belong to, we are all God's beloved children. God is our Father, but he is not like human fathers. God is not a human like us. *"God is not a man, that he should lie, nor is he the Son of Man, that he should change his mind. Does he speak then not act? Does he promise and not fulfill?" (Num. 23:19)* The answer to both those rhetorical questions is no. God is not like us. He is infinitely better and holy in every sense of the word. He made all, knows all, and sees all. *"From heaven the Lord looks down and sees ALL mankind" (Ps. 33:13; emphasis mine).*

God is omnipotent, which means he has unlimited power and can do whatever he wants. God answers to no one. God is all-powerful, and all of creation answers to him. *"Even from eternity I am he, and there is none who can deliver out of my hand; I act and who can reverse it?" (Isa. 43:13).* His power is not restricted or bound by anything. There is no person or force that exists that can counteract God's will. God is truth, and he can be trusted. *"Every word of God is flawless; he is a shield to those who take refuge in him" (Prov. 30:5).*

God is three persons in one. He exists in the trinity, God the Father, the Son (Jesus), and the Holy Spirit. Jesus is called the Word in the Bible. *"In the beginning was the Word, and the Word was with God and the Word was God" (John 1:1).* Because humans could not follow God's way and kept falling away from him, God became a man, Jesus, and came to earth to reveal himself to us and teach us how to love like he loves and to better help us see and understand God's true nature. *"The Word became flesh and dwelt among us" (John 1:14).* Jesus tells us that if we know him, we know God because he is God. Jesus said, *"I and the Father are one" (John 10:30).*

After mankind rejected God himself yet again and put Jesus to death by crucifixion, he rose from the dead fulfilling the scripture and proving he was in fact God. Because God knew that mankind cannot be holy or righteous on our own, he promised to help us. Jesus promised to send his spirit back to live inside all believers. God is the Holy Spirit, our helper. *"God is spirit, and his worshippers must worship in spirit and in truth" (John 4:24).* God sent himself in the form of the Holy Spirit to live and dwell inside everyone who follows him, to help guide us to walk with him and be faithful to God. *"Because God has poured out his love into our hearts by the Holy Spirit, whom he has given us" (Rom. 5:5).* In fact, the Holy Spirit is so integral to our spiritual health Jesus actually told his disciples that it was better for all of us if he left us and went to be with God in heaven because then his spirit would be with all believers forever. *"But I tell you the truth: It is good for you that I am going away. Unless I go away, the Counselor will not come to you: But if I go, I will send him to you… But when he, the Spirit of Truth, comes he will guide you into all truth. He will not speak on his own; he will speak only what he hears, and he will tell you what is to come" (John 16:7, 13).* God gives us believers his mighty counselor inside us always to guide us and lead us through life.

God is love. *"God is love. Whoever lives in love lives in God and God in him" (1 John 4:16).* Love is who God is and what he wants from us his children. He wants us to truly love our fellow brothers and sisters because he loves them. He wants us to show love by using his words and teachings and the example Jesus set when he walked the earth. *"Love comes from God. Everyone who loves has been born of God and knows God. Whoever does not love does not know God, because God is love. This is how God showed his love for us; He sent his one and only son into the world that we may LIVE through him" (1 John 4:7–9; emphasis mine).* The love of God is a pure, unconditional, no-strings-attached love. You cannot earn the love of God; it is freely given to all creation. It is not based on anything you can say, think, or do. God's love is eternal. Love is all we will take with us when we leave this earth one day and transition to our eternal life.

God is light. *"God is light, in him there is no darkness at all" (1 John 1:5).* In fact, the book of Revelation describes heaven as not needing any light at all except God and Jesus themselves to illuminate all of heaven. No sun, no moon, no stars are required in heaven. It is pure, unfiltered light from the glory that radiates from our God. *"The city does not need the sun or the moon to shine on it, for the glory of God gives it light and the lamb is the lamp" (Rev. 21:23).* Jesus says he is light, and we are called to be light to the world as well. *"Then Jesus again spoke to them saying, 'I am the light of the world; he who follows me will not walk in darkness but have the light of life'" (John 8:12).*

When true believers are present, God is there, and his light is present shining through them, and no forces of evil or darkness can stand in his holy presence. *"The lights shines in the darkness and the darkness has NOT overcome it" (John 1:5; emphasis mine).* That means that when we accept God in our lives, we have his light inside us and no forces of evil will be too great or powerful to overtake us. *"For you were formerly darkness, but now you are light in the Lord; walk as children of light" (Eph. 5:8).* God wants us to shine brightly to those around us to draw others to him and cast out the darkness in the world. Jesus instructed us to *"let your light shine before men that they may see your good works and glorify your Father in heaven" (Matt. 5:16).*

God is our helper in every and any circumstance. *"God is our refuge and strength and ever-present help in times of trouble" (Ps. 46:1).* God is the giver of life and the sustainer of life. "*Surely God is my help; the Lord is the one who sustains me" (Ps. 54:4).* Truly God is the one allowing you to stay alive at any given moment. God sustains the beating of your heart and the breath in your lungs. God provides and sustains life in all things. God is our savior. *"Praise be to the Lord, to God our savior, who daily bears our burdens. Our God is a God who saves; from the sovereign Lord comes escape from death" (Ps. 68:19–20).* It is God who will decide where you will spend eternity; your acceptance of Jesus is where that decision lies.

God is just and righteous, and he always does what is good and what is right. *"The Lord is gracious and righteous; our God is full of compassion" (Ps. 116:5).* God is fair. *"For the Lord your God is God of gods and Lord of lords, the great God, mighty and awesome, who shows no partiality and accepts no bribes" (Deut. 10:17).* God is our judge. God is the one we need to answer to and will be held accountable to one day when our life here on earth ends. *"The heavens proclaim his righteousness, for God himself is judge" (Ps. 50:6).* God is peace. *"For God is not a God of disorder but of peace" (1 Cor. 14:33).* God is loving and compassionate. *"The Lord is compassionate and gracious. Slow to anger and abounding in steadfast love and faithfulness" (Exod. 34:6).* God is faithful and trustworthy and keeps his promises always. He shows us mercy and gives us forgiveness. *"For the Lord your God is a merciful God; he will not abandon or destroy you or forget the covenant with your forefathers, which he confirmed to them by oath" (Deut. 4:31).*

It now makes slightly more sense when God says "I am who I am" because he is trying to convey that he is infinite and lord over all things. He has always been and will always be. God answers to no one, but all of creation answers to him. Only by reading his Word and discovering the truth of who God really is through Scripture and discovering for yourself through a relationship with him will this all begin to unfold in our minds and make sense.

The Word of God

L ET'S START OFF BY understanding how important the Word of God is. God gave us the Bible, also called Scripture, which are his words, written by man but divinely inspired by God. It is written by both man and God as a collaborative manual for how to live our lives and what God created us each for. *"In the beginning was the word, and the Word was with God, and the word was God, he was in the beginning with God" (John 1:1–2).* God gave us the Bible as a way to reveal himself to us and allow us to know the truth about who he is and why we were created. God created us to be his eternal family. When all that is written in Scripture comes to full completion and this world as we know it ends, those who chose to hear and accept the Word of God will live in paradise for all eternity with God and other fellow believers. Heaven will be the eternal destination for God's family to live in perfect harmony as God originally intended creation to be. Christians have *"hope of eternal life, which God, who never lies, promised before the ages began" (Titus 1:2).*

Scripture tells the story of our creation by our heavenly Father and of humanities' divine interactions with the living God. The purpose is to teach about who God is and his great love for all his creation, especially us his children. The Word of God is so important that God says that it's his Word, not food or water, that sustains us and gives us life. *"Man does not live on bread alone but on EVERY WORD that comes from the mouth of the Lord" (Deut. 8:3; emphasis mine).* God wants us to hunger and thirst for his Word and for TRUTH. It is estimated that over 5–6 billion copies have been printed in over seven hundred different languages. The Bible has stood the test of time; it is the most read book on the planet. It is truth. The Bible is meant to be read from start to finish and meant to be read over and over again throughout your lifetime. It is meant to be pondered on, studied, talked about, and thought about. God's Word is true and reliable, and he has answers for all our life's questions (big and small) in his Word. God covers and addresses every issue that humanity has ever or will ever face. God has equipped each of us with the tools we need to navigate this life here on earth and prepare our hearts and souls to be with him one day in heaven for all eternity.

When you feel lost or in the dark and you need direction, God's Word is there to guide you and light the way. ***"Your word is a lamp to my feet and a light to my path" (Ps. 119:105).*** The Bible is our manual and road map. The Bible is an amazing masterpiece and the best story ever told. ***"The wisdom that comes from heaven is first of all pure, then peace-loving, considerate, submissive, full of mercy and good fruit, impartial and sincere" (James 3:17).*** It is full of amazing miracles and great signs and wonders. It is full of love, forgiveness, mercy, and passion. It is full of epic battles and amazing victories. It is full of unbelievable promises that always come to fulfillment in the most amazing, unfathomable way. The Bible shows God's constant attempt to have a relationship with the people he created and the repetitive turning away from God by humanity. It shows God reaching out time and time again and being rejected over and over. In spite of humanities' disobedience, God never gives up on us, and he will continually reach out throughout all generations in history and lovingly forgive anyone who turns away from sin and turns back to God. Because of God's great love for his creation, there is always hope for mankind because even ***"if we are unfaithful, he will remain faithful, for he cannot deny himself" (2 Tim. 2:13).***

The Bible is divided into the Old Testament and the New Testament. The Old Testament predicts the coming of Jesus Christ to defeat death and sin once and for all. The New Testament tells of the fulfillment of prophecy about the coming of Jesus Christ, his death, resurrection, and ascension into heaven. Jesus's death forms a new covenant between God and all of humanity for all of eternity.

Jesus's birth, ministry, death, and resurrection do not eradicate the Old Testament scripture, replace it, or make it irrelevant. Instead, Jesus fulfills scripture. Jesus's death and resurrection fulfill God's promises in the Old Testament and validate that Jesus was God himself and vindicate that his mission to rescue humanity, once and for all, from the forces of evil has been accomplished and his work is complete. Jesus never denied or rebuked the Old Testament; he knew it and he affirmed it. Even though God has made a new covenant with us all through the bloodshed of Jesus Christ, it is still important to know and understand the Old Testament. God is the same God he has always been. *"I the Lord do not change" (Mal. 3:6).* Therefore, all of scripture is relevant. *"Your word, Lord, is eternal; it stands firm in the heavens" (Ps. 119:89).*

The Old Testament and the Bible as a whole serve as our history lesson of what works and what doesn't, what to do and what not to do. This is why God tells us to know his Word so we can know how to live according to his will. *"I have hidden your word in my heart, so that I might now sin against you" (Ps. 119:11).* The Bible is full of stories of men and women just like you and me who have real-life struggles, just like you and me. The Bible highlights the many stories of people who tried to follow God but failed on their own. Only the men and women that recognized who God truly is and fully put their faith in him and relied on his strength and wisdom, not their own, were successful in achieving amazing feats. The Bible is full of stories of how God can redeem anyone who commits their life to following him and that there is no one he can't use to accomplish his will. No sin is too great to separate you from the love and mercy of God, and no person is too far lost. In fact, some of the men and women he used most effectively were considered great sinners: murderers (Moses, David, Saul later known as the Apostle Paul), prostitutes (Rahab, Mary Magdeline), tax collectors (Matthew, Zaccheus), and others society would have viewed as sinners. It is never too late to turn your life over to God, receive his mercy, and start over as his child on mission for his kingdom. God offers free salvation to all who accept his son, Jesus Christ.

God's Word details the life and ministry of his Son Jesus. Jesus is the exact replica of our God. ***"The son is the image of the invisible God… For God was pleased to have ALL his fullness dwell in him" (Col. 1:15, 19; emphasis mine).*** Jesus lived his life as an example to us to demonstrate how to love God and love others through his perfect obedience to God's will. The New Testament Gospels of Matthew, Mark, Luke, and John are all firsthand accounts of the life and ministry of Jesus Christ. His teachings show us who God really is and what is important to him. Not only did Jesus teach us what God wants and expects from us, but he also modeled how to live that out. He was both fully God and fully man, yet he never sinned. God knows you and I are not capable of living that perfect life of obedience, so he sent Jesus to die for us all so that our sins may be forgiven and so we could be made right in God's eyes. ***"Jesus answered, 'I am the way and the truth and the life. No one comes to the father except through me'" (John 14:6).***

The Bible is filled with beautiful promises that God faithfully offers to all who love him. If you're a Christian, reading Scripture is vital to the health of your relationship with your heavenly Father. God doesn't reveal all of himself at once to us. But he draws us deeper into relationship and reveals more of himself, his glory, and his power in your life the more you abide in his Word. Just like any human relationship, spending time together is what grows the relationship faster than anything else. This is the same for your walk with God. The more time you spend reading the Word of God and talking to God in prayer and praise, the closer you will become and the more you will recognize God's works in your life and fully receive the blessings he wants to bestow on you. You must humble yourself and realize you have much to learn and gain from reading Scripture. When you read Scripture with a totally open mind and open heart to receive God's revelation, Scripture will unfold in a new understandable way to you. Reading the word is just the first step. ***"Therefore, get rid of all moral filth and the evil that is so prevalent and humbly accept the word planted in you, which can save you. Do not merely listen to the word, and so deceive yourselves. Do what it says" (James 1:21–22).***

God calls Christians to action. He wants you to not only read his words but truly think about them and take them to heart and allow his truth to wash over you and change you. God wants to nurture your heart, mind, and soul in a way that only he can. There is truly no one else or anything else in this world that can satisfy your soul like God can. God designed us with a longing to know him. Anyone that doesn't know God will always be searching for something to fill the void that God created you to have without him. God wants you to search for him, and he promises that when you search for him, you will find him. ***"You will seek me and find me when you seek me with all your heart" (Jer. 29:13).***

In order to fully benefit from all that scripture has to reveal to you, God wants us to study his Word in depth. Bible studies are excellent ways to dig deep into scripture to reveal more meaning. Discussing God's Word with others also helps to show you how God speaks differently to different people. You should meditate on the Lord's word. By this I mean really think about the words you are reading. Let them penetrate and change your mind and heart. ***"The book of the law should not depart from your mouth, but you should meditate on it day and night, so that you may be careful to do according to all that is written in it. For then you will make your way prosperous, and then you will have good success" (Josh. 1:8).***

Knowing God's Word is key to doing what is right. If you don't know what God expects of you and calls you to do, you can never live out your true purpose on this earth. Many people say that they find the Bible hard to read and hard to understand. Beginning to read the Bible can be a little intimidating at first. There are many translations of the Bible that are easy to read, and finding one that assists you with beginning to seek him is key. I personally love to look at different translations and versions to better dissect meaning from God's Word. I used many different translations in the writing of this book to help convey God's perfect word in a way that I feel allows us to see the big picture of God's truth most clearly. When I first began reading Scripture, I also felt it was hard to understand and confusing at points, but then I prayed that God would give me fresh eyes to see his truth through his Word. ***"The unfolding of your word gives light; it imparts understanding to the simple" (Ps. 119:130).*** I prayed to have a fresh mind to understand God and what he has for my life. It was almost like a light bulb went off, and all of a sudden, I could clearly understand God's plan for humanity and the crazy beautiful love story that is the Bible. I have no doubt that God will do the same for each and every one of you if you ask him to! Ask his Holy Spirit to guide you and impart understanding to you when you read Scripture. God loves all people, and he wants nothing more than for all his children to know him, turn back to him, and love him.

Many people think that the Bible is outdated and no longer relevant to today's society. God, however, tells us that his Word is everlasting and always relevant. ***"The grass withers and the flowers fall, but the word of God endures forever" (Isa. 40:8).*** We've all heard that those who don't know history are doomed to repeat it. This is so true and is the reason that knowing the truth about the history of God's creation and interaction with mankind is vital to moving God's kingdom forward and not falling prey to the same traps Satan has been setting for God's people since the beginning of time. God says, ***"What has been, will be again, what has been done will be done again; there is nothing new under the sun" (Eccles. 1:9).*** The truth is God's Word addresses most of every situation one could ever find themselves in. The Word of God is just as relevant today as it was thousands of years ago. And the God of the universe is working the same in the world today as he was back in biblical times. He is still moving and using men and women all over the world to accomplish his will. ***"Your word, Lord, is eternal; it stands firm in the heavens. Your faithfulness continues through all generations; you established the earth; and it endures. Your law endures to this day, for all things serve you" (Ps. 119:89–91).***

We know this is true because we know our God is eternal and never changes. ***"For I the Lord do not change" (Mal. 1:8).*** Since Jesus is God's Son, we know ***"Jesus Christ is the same yesterday, today and forever" (Heb. 13:8).*** I don't want us to make the mistake of putting God in a box and think that we know everything we need to know about him from the Bible. That is untrue. God does not exist in the finite constraints that man exists in. God defies all man-made parameters of time and space. There is no way for us to fully comprehend just how powerful our God is. What seems impossible by man's standards are a nonissue for God. He literally controls everything, and everything exists only because he allows it to. Jesus tells us, **"With man, this is impossible, but with God ALL things are possible" (Matt. 19:26; emphasis mine).** Even though the Bible is done being compiled, it is impossible to record every miracle God has performed for every human throughout history. We will never fully know just how awesome God is and all the amazing ways he has intervened for humanity throughout time. We still have much to learn about God and his kingdom. God is faithful to reveal his glory and give answers to those who seek them. **"Call to me and I will answer you and show you great and mighty things you have not known before" (Jer. 33:3).** God will always be a great mystery, but God speaks and moves very powerfully in all humans that invite him in.

Just as God is very real and he is our protection and source of life, we have an enemy who is very real as well, Satan. Satan was a jealous angel that tried to make himself above God. Because of his pride, he was cast out of heaven. Jesus told his disciples, **"I watched Satan fall from heaven like lightning" (Luke 10:18).** After he was banned from heaven, he has made his dwelling place here on earth, and he is very busy trying to steal souls and all of mankind's rightful inheritance to eternal life with God.

Satan is jealous of you, and he hates you! He is your true enemy. He knows all the goodness that God has in store for each of us, and he knows that his final destination is the pit of hell. Misery loves company, and so Satan will do whatever it takes to steal as many souls away from God as he can. Satan is a liar, and he wants nothing more than to separate you from God. His only agenda is for you to spend eternity with him and not with God where you belong. Scary thought, right? The good news is, however, he can't take your godly inheritance if you don't willingly give it up! But we must be vigilant to guard ourselves from all his deceit and deception. This famous quote by Tucker Max says it all, "The devil doesn't come to you dressed in a red cape and pointy horns but disguised as everything you ever wanted." Satan knows your desires and your weaknesses, and he will use those against you to suck you in and lead you astray. He will use any and every trick he can to keep you from knowing your identity as a child of God and the inheritance that awaits you when your life here on this earth ends. He uses everything in this world as a tool to distract us and keep us busy so we can't learn the truth about who God is and who he created each of us to be. This is the reason that reading your Bible and knowing the truth of scripture is critical. If you are truly going to follow Christ on this earth, you must know what he taught. If you are going to do as all Christians are called to do and share the good news of Christ and try and bring many to the kingdom of God, you must know God's promises. *"All scripture is God-breathed and is useful for teaching, rebuking, correcting, and training in righteousness, so that the servant of God may be thoroughly equipped for every good work (2 Tim. 3:16–17).*

Paul tells us in the letter to the church in Ephesus, *"Finally be strong in the Lord and in his mighty power. Put on the full armor of God, so that you can take your stand against the devil's schemes. For our struggle is not against flesh and blood, but against the rulers, against the authorities, against the powers of the dark world and against spiritual forces of evil in the heavenly realms. Therefore, put on the full armor of God, so that when the day of evil comes, you may be able to stand your ground… Stand firm then, with the belt of truth buckled around your waist, with the breastplate of righteousness in place, and with your feet fitted with the readiness that comes from the gospel of peace. In addition to all of this, take up the shield of faith, with which you can extinguish all the flames of the evil one. Take the helmet of salvation and the sword of the spirit, which is the word of God"* (Eph. 6:10–17).

Scripture tells us the weapon of choice to defeat Satan is the Word of God. Scripture is our sword to defeat evil. God is telling us that other humans are not our enemies even though Satan tries to make you think they are. He loves division and conflict and wars. He wants us to hate our fellow man and be intolerant of one another.

God reveals the truth of who our true enemy is though; it's Satan and all the powers of darkness in the spiritual realm. That is who we are to go to battle against. When you know the Word of God, Satan can't trick you into sin. *"I have stored up your word in my heart, that I might not sin against you" (Ps. 119:11).*

Scripture is powerful; it is always relevant to all people living at any given time in any given place. *"For the word of God is living and active, sharper than any two-edged sword, piercing to the division of soul and of spirit, of joints and of marrow, and discerning the thoughts and intentions of the heart" (Heb. 4:12).* Now that's powerful! When you know the truth of what God says about himself, his Son Jesus, you, and his plan for you, Satan's tricks no longer work! That is why Satan tries so hard to keep us distracted from walking with God. Satan uses many things to distract us and fill our minds with his lies (just look at our entertainment industry). He knows if he can get you to believe the lie that there is no God or that there are many gods or, worse yet, that you can be your own god, he knows he can cause you to stumble and fall farther away from truth and salvation. There is a new phrase that has surfaced in recent years, "my truth" and "living my truth"; well, friends, that's a lie and trap from Satan as well. There is no individual truth; there is only *the* truth. If you don't know *the* truth, you will fall for the lies of this world. Satan wants to bombard you with lies so it starts to distort the words of God and the truth found in the Bible. Satan has done a great job of causing chaos and confusion in this world.

Luckily for us, Satan isn't creative like our God. He has been using the same playbook since the beginning of time. Satan has been using the same tricks on all humanity since Adam and Eve. First, he tries to make you doubt God, then he tries to get you to disobey God. Finally, he will try to get you to deny God. Satan tries to convince you that God is not an all-knowing, all-loving good God who knows you personally and is available to you personally whenever you seek him. God is not a far-off, distant God who passively sits back and watches us suffer. God comes to the rescue of anyone who invites him into their hearts and minds and welcomes in his Son, Jesus. God can be accessed 24-7 with any request or any cry for help with just a simple thought. Our God is everywhere all the time. *"The eyes of the Lord are in every place keeping watch on the evil and the good" (Prov. 15:3).* He is all-knowing and all-powerful. *"And no creature is hidden from his sight, but all are naked and exposed to the eyes of him to whom we must give account" (Heb. 4:13).*

Nothing is hidden from God, including our struggle with sin. God is our help though. God knows the traps Satan has set for you in your life and the ones he plans for your future. If you call to God for deliverance, his promise is that he will deliver you. *"He has delivered us from the domain of the darkness and transferred us to the kingdom of his beloved son" (Col. 1:13).* If you call to God to protect you from Satan, his promise is that he will. *"We know that everyone who has been born of God does not keep on sinning, but he who was born of God protects him, and the evil one does not touch him" (1 John 5:18).*

When we study the Word of God and understand who God is, we can see Satan coming! It is written that God has already defeated Satan for all eternity. Satan has no power over you IF you don't allow him to. *"How great is the goodness you have stored up for those who fear you. You lavish it on those who come to you for protection, blessing them before the watching world. You hide them in the shelter of your presence, safe from those who conspire against them. You shelter them in your presence, far from accusing tongues" (Ps. 31:19–20).* Trust me when I say, Satan is ALWAYS conspiring against you! God is your only shelter and protection from him. We can fight against Satan and the powers of darkness by knowing the Word of God and letting that be our sword to defend ourselves and defeat the enemy of our souls. Fear is Satan's oldest and most effective tactic. When fear and anxiety creep in, remember what God's Word says, *"Do not be anxious about anything, but in everything, by prayer and petition, with thanksgiving, present your requests to God. And the peace which transcends all understanding, will guard your hearts and your minds in Christ Jesus" (Phil. 4:6–7).* Jesus many times told us not to worry. God will take care of you and meet all your needs when you abide in him. *"Can anyone of you by worrying add a single hour to your life? Therefore, do not worry about tomorrow, for tomorrow will worry about itself. Each day has enough trouble of its own" (Matt. 6:27, 34).*

If you truly believe that Jesus died for your sins so that you will have eternal life in heaven with God forever no matter what trials you endured on this earth, what on earth could possibly give you any worry or anxiety? Jesus warned us that we would have problems in life. *"I have told you these things so that IN ME you may have peace. In this world you will have trouble. But take heart! I have over-come this world" (John 16:33; emphasis mine).* Jesus didn't say you might have some trouble. He boldly says you WILL have trouble. We live in a broken world full of sin all around us, but the good news is this life is temporary. We need to stop living for this world and start living for eternity.

Eternal life will be in one of two very real places, heaven or hell. You get to decide where you will spend it. When you put eternity with or without God into perspective, all fear of man and circumstances here on earth should be gone. *"So we can confidently say, 'The Lord is my helper, I will not fear; what can man do to me?'" (Heb. 13:6).* We can't afford to be living with a spirit of fear or worrying about pleasing others and conforming to the sinful world around us. The Bible instructs us, *"Do not conform to the patterns of this world. But be transformed by the renewing of your mind. Then you will be able to test and approve what God's will is- his good pleasing and perfect will" (Rom. 12:2).* Conforming to the world around you and allowing the things and people of this world to be your guide instead of God is a deadly mistake. Remember, Satan is the ruler of THIS earthly world. Jesus refers to Satan *"as the prince of this world"* in *John 12:31, 14:30 and 16:11*.

While Satan has limited power on this earth for a time, God has power over all for all eternity. Only God can transform and renew your mind. I believe reading the Word of God is the key to that transformation. Before Jesus left this world, he prayed to God and asked God to *"sanctify them by the truth; your word is truth" (John 17:17).* Knowing the Word of God is knowing truth. Knowing God's good will and knowing your part in helping it all come together is where you begin. Only then can you start to apply it to your daily life and interactions with others.

When you read about the life that Jesus lived and the love he showed the world, you can't help but be renewed with a fresh sense of joy. You can't help but be transformed and want to be a better person and treat others with the love that you feel bursting inside you. We need to set our minds and hearts on serving the one who truly matters. *"Set your minds on the things that are above, not on things that are on the earth" (Col. 3:2).* Let all the cares of this world be far from your mind and focus on the truth of who God is. The rest is all distractions designed by Satan to separate us from our Creator. The things of the world are temporary, and most are not from God but from our enemy. *"Do not love the world or anything in the world. If anyone loves the world, the love of the Father is not in them. For everything in the world—the lust of the flesh, the lust of the eyes, and the pride of life—comes not from the Father but from the world. The world and its desires pass away, but whoever does the will of God lives forever" (1 John 2:15–17).* Our hope and salvation comes from Jesus alone. *"For there is one God, and there is one mediator between God and men, the man Jesus Christ" (1 Tim. 2:5).* All hope and faith should be in your one and only ticket to heaven, Jesus Christ. This is the good news of the gospel!

Jesus Is the Way

JESUS IS THE SON of God but also God himself since God exists as three persons/entities in one. Jesus confirmed, *"I and the Father are one" (John 10:30).* Jesus is our God sent to earth to live among us in human form in order to teach us truth. Jesus is the fulfillment of the scriptures about the messiah God would send to save humanity once and for all. *"For to us a child is born, to us a son is given; and the government shall be upon his shoulders, and his name shall be called Wonderful Counselor, Mighty God, Everlasting Father, Prince of Peace" (Isa. 9:6).* God knew that we could simply not live a holy life because of the sin and darkness that had entered the world through human disobedience and the forces of evil that oppose him in the unseen realm. Because of this, God lovingly sent his Son Jesus into the world in order to show us himself and the truth. *"And the word became flesh and dwelt among us, and we have seen his glory, glory as of the only son from the father, full of grace and truth" (John 1:14).*

Jesus came humbly to this earth as a baby; he grew up in the same world full of sin that we live in. He experienced all the emotions and things in life that we experience. He felt hunger, he felt pain, he felt sadness, rejection, humiliation, betrayal, anxiety, and all the other negative feelings humans feel. Jesus gladly did this so he could fully understand and sympathize with our human condition. *"For we do not have a high priest who is unable to empathize with our weaknesses, but we have one who has been tempted in every way, just as you are yet he did not sin" (Heb. 4:15).* God did not send Jesus to punish us but to save us from ourselves and to defeat Satan and the powers of darkness once and for all. *"For God did NOT send his son into the world to condemn the world, but in order that the world might be saved through him" (John 3:17; emphasis mine).* Jesus did not come to point fingers and accuse us humans of not living up to God's standards. Instead, he came to find the lost and those farthest from God and bring them back home to the Father. Jesus spent much of his time with those on the fringes of society, the people many thought irrelevant and too far gone. This is the reason so many religious leaders in Jesus's time disliked him and tried to discredit him and put him to death. *"But the Pharisees and the teachers of the law who belonged to their sect complained to his disciples, 'Why do you eat and drink with tax collectors and sinners?' Jesus answered them, 'It is not the healthy who need a doctor, but the sick. I have not come to call the righteous, but sinners to repentance'" (Luke 5:30–33).*

God loves all his children, and so Jesus came to save all. Jesus was sent as our savior! Jesus is our perfect role model and teacher on how God wants us to live and love. *"In this, the love of God was made manifest among us, that God sent his only son into the world, so that we might live through him" (1 John 4:9).* God showed us his perfect love in the form of Jesus. God was showing us through the life of Jesus how to live as he intended humanity to be in the beginning. King Jesus lived the exact opposite of how earthly kings behave and rule. Jesus came as a servant, not as a powerful king or ruler. *"Who, being in very nature God, did not consider equality with God something to be used to his own advantage; rather, he made himself nothing by taking the very nature of a servant, being made in human likeness. And being found in appearance as a man, he humbled himself by becoming obedient to death, even death on a cross!" (Phil. 2:5–11).* Jesus was humble in heart and in spirit, and he showed the world how God's kingdom is drastically different that earthly kingdoms. He taught that service to others and selfless acts of love is what will elevate you in the kingdom of God.

If you are searching for anything in this life, for meaning, purpose, the way to go or live, and the path to follow, look no further.

Jesus is the way. Jesus said, *"I am the way, the truth, and the life: no one comes to the Father except through me" (John 14:6).* If you don't already know Jesus as your personal savior and his glorious gift of forgiveness and eternal life, I hope you keep reading and discover absolute truth for the first time ever. If you already know Jesus, it's time to start getting serious about your walk with him. Us Christians need a wake-up call. This is a call to action to start taking the kingdom back for God. Satan is alive and well on planet Earth, and he is rapidly eroding away the goodness God has created. Through the sins of mankind, we are destroying God's beautiful Earth, perverting what he says is good and hurting our fellow man. God gave everything to us when he gave us Christ Jesus. Jesus is the ONLY WAY that we could ever be right with God. *"And there is salvation in no one else, for there is no other name under heaven given among men by which we must be saved" (Acts 4:12).*

Jesus took all the sins of the world on his shoulders and died to make us right with God. Jesus didn't just simply die on the cross; he was brutalized, tortured, betrayed, shunned, shamed, humiliated, laughed at, spit on, hated, and horrifically murdered for our sake. *"But he was pierced for our transgressions, he was crushed for our iniquities; the punishment that brought us peace was on him, and by his wounds we are healed. We all, like sheep, have gone astray, each of us has turned to our own way; and the Lord has laid on him the iniquity of us all. He was oppressed and afflicted, yet he did not open his mouth; he was led like a lamb to the slaughter, and as a sheep before its shears is silent, so he did not open his mouth" (Isa 53:5–7).*

Jesus endured all this to show us just how much God loves us. It is perfect sacrificial love. *"Greater love has no one than this, that someone lay down his life for his friends" (John 15:13).* Jesus died for ALL mankind. Past, present, and future generations. Not a single one of us deserve God's grace. We deserve punishment for our sins, but our good Father forgives. *"For the wage of sin is death, but the GIFT of God is eternal life in Christ Jesus our Lord" (Rom. 6:23).* We don't deserve forgiveness, but God freely gives it to us anyway because of his great love for his creation. *"He does not treat us as our sins deserve or repay us according to our iniquities. For as high as the heavens are above the earth, so great is his love for those who fear him" (Ps. 103:10–11).*

God's forgiveness is available to all who accept the free gift of salvation through faith in Jesus. Your only job is to believe these words and to accept the gift. That is truly all it takes to be right with God. It only requires you to admit to God that you are a sinner and that you need a savior to be right with him. Then you must believe Jesus is that savior and accept that Jesus died for you to pay for those sins. That's it; it's that simple! *"Because, if you confess with your mouth that Jesus is Lord and believe in your heart that God raised him from the dead, you will be saved" (Rom. 10:9).* You could never do anything to earn salvation. It is 100 percent free. *"For by grace you have been saved THROUGH FAITH. And this is not your own doing; it is the gift of God, not a result of works, so that no one may boast" (Eph. 2:8–9; emphasis mine).*

It is our faith in Jesus that saves us. It is a gift from a God who loves you and adores you and doesn't want to spend an eternity without you. But since he is such a good, good Father, he lets you make that choice. Free will is a crucial point I do not want you to miss. He doesn't force himself on you or on anyone else for that matter. He allows you to choose to follow him and love him and have eternal life with him OR to lead your own way through this life and suffer the consequences of eternal separation from him in the next life. Free will is given to all humans, and it extends into eternal life. God always welcomes all into his loving family. He forgives all who ask for forgiveness. He never brings your forgiven transgressions up again. *"The Lord is compassionate and gracious, slow to anger, abounding in love. He does not treat us as our sins deserve or repay us according to our iniquities. As far as the east is from the west, so far has he removed our transgressions from us" (Ps. 103:8, 10, 12–13).* You are washed clean by the blood of Jesus the minute you confess he is your Lord and Savior. *"For God so LOVED the WORLD, that he gave his only son, that whoever believes in him should not perish but have eternal life. For God did NOT send his son into the world to condemn the world, but in order that the world may be*

SAVED through HIM. WHOEVER BELIEVES in HIM is not condemned"
(John 3:16–17; emphasis mine).

Notice God says whoever. Jesus's death made it possible for us all to be reconciled with our Creator. This applies to every person that has ever and will ever walk this earth. This is the good news of the gospel! This is the new covenant between God and his people. God's promises are no longer only for his chosen Israelites. This invitation is now extended to all people. It's for you and for me and for everyone we both know. It is our job as Christians to make sure everyone we know gets the message. If you have family, friends, coworkers, neighbors, or anyone else you know who doesn't know Christ, it's time to start getting serious about doing God's will. It is our duty to bring the good news of Jesus to our fellow man. Jesus said, ***"Therefore go and make disciples of all nations, baptizing them in the name of the Father and of the son and of the Holy Spirit and teaching them to obey everything that I have commanded you. And surely, I am with you always, to the very end of the age" (Matt. 28:19–20).***

You are either on team Jesus or you aren't. There is no middle ground. We are told that Jesus will come back one day, and when he does, it will be too late to choose a side. ***"So Christ, having been offered once to bear the sins of many, will appear a second time, not to deal with sin but to save those who are eagerly waiting for him" (Heb. 9:28).*** When Jesus comes back again, it will only be to collect his chosen followers and bring them to eternal life with him forever. He is not coming again to try to convince people of the truth. He already did this once. The good news and truth of the gospel is already being preached most everywhere. Your mind needs to already be made up. Your heart and soul need to already be ready for the second coming of Christ, which could be literally any second. ***"Therefore, you must always be ready, for the Son of Man is coming at an hour you do not expect" (Matt. 24:44).*** Only God knows the details of when that will be or what that will look like.

"But concerning that day and hour no one knows, not even the angels of Heaven, nor the son, but the father only" (Matt. 24:36). But God gives us several warnings that it could be any time, and we should always be alert. Jesus says, ***"Be on the alert, for you***

do not know which day your Lord is coming" (Matt. 24:42). I'll elaborate on that later.

God has given us fair warning and notice and plenty of time (2023 years to be exact) to decide to be on the side of truth. When Jesus comes back, it will be to gather his elect, not to try and convince those who have rejected him. *"For the Lord himself will descend from heaven with a cry of command, with the voice of an archangel and with the sound of the trumpet of God. And the dead in Christ will rise first. Then we who are alive, who are left, will be caught up together with them in the clouds to meet the Lord in the air, and so we will always be with the Lord" (1 Thess. 4:16–17).* This is the beautiful promise God gives to all who love him and accept Jesus as their Savior. This is your guarantee when you accept Jesus.

Identity

Knowing your true identity as a child of the Most High King is the key to walking into your purpose and calling in life. We were each created uniquely and beautiful by our heavenly Father, and God has specific plans for your life. Recognizing that and walking into it is your choice though. ***"For we are his workmanship, created in Christ Jesus for good works, which God prepared beforehand, that we should walk in them" (Eph. 2:10).*** We all want to be known and feel seen. We all want to be loved for who we truly are inside. Good news, you are already fully loved and accepted by your Creator. But because we are humans, we want people to like us.

Most people will search their whole lives for the approval of others. Sadly, we often use other people's opinions of us dictate how we feel about ourselves, shape who we become, and how we respond to the world around us. We are all searching this world in all the wrong places for what God already freely gave us: love and acceptance. Many of the mental health struggles people all over the world are dealing with, I believe, have a common underlying problem, a false sense of identity. When you don't know your true identity in Christ as a child of God, Satan can use this world and all his lies and schemes to give you a false identity. This false identity will wreak havoc on your mental health. We are constantly labeled our whole lives by others. Sometimes by things we choose and sometimes by things we can't control. Whether it's by our physical appearances, like height, weight, hair color, skin color, age, etc., or by societal status and economic ranks, humans will find a way to label each other based on a limitless criteria. We have been labeled by society since the moment we are born. We are labeled throughout our entire lives by the world around us. Things like our interests, our intellect, our careers, our choices, the company we keep, etc. We are labeled by things we can control, too, like our temperaments and our reactions to life's challenges. I'm sure you can think of a million other ways that we label each other and ourselves. Luckily, God is not a human, and he does not look at our outward appearances or talents to decide our worth. *"God sees not as man sees, for man looks at the outward appearance, but the Lord looks at the heart" (1 Sam. 16:7).*

The point is when you don't know God is your father, you begin to believe all the labels, false or otherwise, that people have said about you. It is a trick Satan uses to get us to not step into or live out our full potential and calling for God's kingdom. God has a plan for each and every one of us. *"For I know the plans I have for you declares the Lord, plans to prosper you and not to harm you, plans to give you a hope and a future" (Jer. 29:11).* You are a child of God, and nothing anyone else says about you matters or defines who you are. You don't have to pretend to be something you are not around God to receive his great love. He already knows everything about you, the good and the bad, and he loves you all the same. It is so refreshing to know that you can simply come to God as you are. You don't need to fix yourself up or cover yourself up to come to God. You can come before God as your fully authentic self and know that no matter what, he loves you dearly. Only God can love with that unconditional love. Only God knows the real you since he created you. *"Before I formed you in the womb I knew you, before you were born I set you apart" (Jer. 1:5).*

We have all been labeled by things that are not truly our identity in life. We've all been called names and thrown insults to our character. When you don't know that God personally knows you and loves you and created you flawlessly, you will buy into the lies of Satan and this world. You will never measure up to the standards of this world. It is an impossible feat. Besides the obvious reason that we are all humans and no one is perfect, the standard is constantly changing. God's standards, however, have always been very simple;

they are constant and eternal standards. *"Love the Lord your God with all your heart and with all your soul and with all your mind. This is the first and greatest commandment. And the second is like it; love your neighbor as yourself"* *(Matt. 22:37–39)*. When your identity is in your salvation in Jesus Christ and your heir as a child of God, nothing else should matter. *"So God created mankind in HIS OWN IMAGE, in the image of God he created them; male and female he created them"* *(Gen. 1:27; emphasis mine)*. This is your true identity. You were created in the image of God, and you are flawless.

When you turn to him and allow him to work in your life as he originally designed and intended your life to be, then your life will be full. When you accept Jesus, you are adopted eternally as a child of God. *"He predestined us for adoption THROUGH Jesus Christ, in accordance with his pleasure and will"* *(Eph. 1:5; emphasis mine)*. Followers of Christ are God's chosen people. *"But to all who did receive him, who believed in his name, he gave the right to become children of God"* *(John 1:12)*. Through that choice, we get our new identity. This is the destiny God had planned for you before he created the world, and he has been patiently waiting for you to discover and step into this beautiful, full life. *"All praise to God, the Father of our Lord Jesus Christ, who has blessed us with every spiritual blessing in the heavenly realms because we are united in Christ. Even BEFORE he made the world, God loved us and CHOSE us in Christ to be holy and without fault in his eyes"* *(Eph. 1:3–4; emphasis mine)*.

The most important part is that we are made holy and righteous in his eyes through the blood of Jesus Christ. There is no other way that any human being can obtain that rightness with God. Jesus is the key. When you decide to accept that, your new identify erases away all the labels and false identity Satan and this world have attached to you. *"Therefore, if ANYONE is in Christ, he is a new creation. The old has passed away; behold, the new has come"* *(2 Cor. 5:17; emphasis mine)*. When you step into your rightful identity as a child of God, you are a totally new creation. *"You are a chosen people, a royal priesthood, a holy nation, God's special possession, that you may declare the praises of him who called you out of darkness into his wonderful light" (1 Pet. 2:9).* We are called out of the darkness of this world and into the glorious light of Christ. When you walk with Christ in your true identity, not only are you walking in light, but you are also the light! Jesus tells us, *"You are the light of the world" (Matt. 5:14).* This is because when you accept Jesus, the Holy Spirit comes and lives inside you. It is no longer you who are in control of your own life and your circumstances, it is the God of the universe. *"It is no longer I who live, but Christ who lives in me. And the life I now live in the flesh I live by faith in the son of God, who loved me and gave himself for me" (Gal. 2:20).*

Because God is in you, you can shine the glory of God to all those around you and help pull others out of darkness. *"Let your light shine before men, that they may see your good works, and glorify your Father which is in heaven" (Matt. 5:16).* Followers of Christ are called to help guide and lead others to truth. So many people are still victims to the lies of the enemy. Christians are supposed to model the love of Christ to all people in a way that helps them discover the God who saves and their own true identity as his children. We are to help show the world that Jesus Christ frees us from the power of Satan. *"If the Son sets you free you are free indeed" (John 8:36).* No one has to live in chains because of sin. No one has to be bound by the weight of darkness. Jesus already defeated sin and death, and he is waiting for us to discover his invitation to join him in this life of true freedom.

Through our adoption as sons and daughters of the Most High King, our blessings, authority, and divine appointments are unlimited. Jesus gave his followers authority over darkness. *"Behold, I have given you authority to tread on serpents and scorpions, and over the power of the enemy, and nothing shall hurt you" (Luke 10:19).* No wonder Satan lies! No wonder he wants you to keep from knowing the truth. Because while the truth sets you free to live out this authority, it binds Satan in chains. Our identity in Christ is powerful! It is so sad that so many people, even Christians, miss that. *"Jesus came and said to them, 'All authority in heaven AND on earth has been given to me'" (Matt. 28:18; emphasis mine).* Thank God I am on team Jesus! Remember, if you are a believer in Christ,

God's Holy Spirit, a.k.a. God, a.k.a. Jesus, lives inside of you! Which means you have authority! *"Little children, you are from God and have overcome them, for he who is in you is greater than he who is in the world" (1 John 4:4).* He who is in us is the God of the universe. Satan is the he who is in the world.

God is greater in EVERY sense of the word, ipso facto YOU are greater. That is your identity. You are a child of God. He is your Father, and he is with you always, and, therefore, you can overcome everything this world (Satan) could possibly throw at you because you have the king of the universe with you always. His unlimited knowledge, time, love, and resources. Satan is no match for you when you roll with Jesus. It's really not even a fair fight for the little guy. This is why Satan will do anything he can to keep you from realizing this truth about your true identity. When you start to discover it, the enemy will undoubtedly start to send "haters" your way. But rest assured once you truly accept God's truth and you stop looking to this world to give you your identity and validation, you will have power over the enemy. Truth is power, and God's Word is truth.

It's All about Love

T HE GREAT MYSTERY OF God and life really isn't a mystery at all. It can all be summed up in one word, love. If you glean nothing else from this book, I hope you at least grasp how critical love is. Love is the answer to every question. Love will never steer you wrong. Love is all that truly matters, and I believe love is all we will take with us when we die. *"Anyone who does not love does not know God, because God is love" (1 John 4:8).* God is love. *"So we have come to know and to believe the love that God has for us, God is love, and whoever abides in love abides in God, and God abides in him" (1 John 4:16).*

God is love, and love is what he wants for us, his creation. God wants us to love him as much as he loves us, and he wants us to love our fellow man as much as God loves them. That is the meaning of life. We are here to learn how to love like Jesus and share the love of God with everyone we meet. We are to prepare our hearts, minds, and souls for eternity with all God's children in heaven living in perfect harmony. This life is practice and spiritual boot camp for the next life. We are to model the love Jesus showed us to others through our words and our actions.

What is love? *"Love is patient, love is kind; love does not envy or boast; it is not arrogant or rude. Love does not insist on its own way; it is not irritable or resentful; it does not rejoice in wrongdoing but rejoices with the truth. Love bears all things, believes all things, hopes all things, endures all things. Love never fails" (1 Cor. 13:4–8).* It is impossible to love our fellow man with this kind of love unless we first love God with all our hearts and all our souls and allow him to fill us with his love. Once we love God first and receive his love, only then do we have enough to overflow love into other's lives. When asked which commandment was the greatest, Jesus answered, *"Love the Lord your God with all your heart and with all your soul and with all your mind. This is the first and greatest commandment. And the second is like it; love your neighbor as yourself. All the other laws of the prophets hang on these two commandments" (Matt. 22:36–40).*

All the Ten Commandments can be broken into the above two groups. The first three commandments are about loving God. The other seven are about loving and respecting others. *"Owe no one anything except to love one another, for he who loves another has fulfilled the law. For the commandments, 'You shall not commit adultery,' 'you shall not commit murder,' 'you shall not steal,' 'you shall not bear false witness,' 'you shall not covet,' are all summed up in the saying 'you shall love your neighbor as yourself.' Love does no harm to a neighbor therefore LOVE is the fulfillment of the law" (Rom. 13:8–10; emphasis mine).* Seems pretty simple when you think about it! This is the golden rule everyone was taught as a child. Treat others how you want to be treated. This is really God's only real rule. If you don't love those God created in the world around you, then you can't possibly truly love God. Put another way, if you don't love and respect what God has made, then you don't fully love and respect God.

Without love, Christianity is meaningless. It doesn't matter how much time or money you donate to charity or how often you go to church or if you read your Bible. If you don't love your fellow man, you are not serving God. The Apostle Paul wrote, *"If I speak in tongues of men or of angels, but do not have love, I am only a resounding gong or a clanging cymbal. If I have the gift of prophecy and can fathom all mysteries and all knowledge and if I have faith that can move mountains, but do not have love, I am nothing. If I give all I possess to the poor and give over my body to hardship that I may boast, but do not have love, I gain nothing" (1 Cor. 13:1–3).* In the same way that *"faith by itself, if it does not have works, is dead... For as the body without the spirit is dead, so faith without works is dead also" (James 2:17, 26)* also so works without love are dead.

Now it is imperative to remember that salvation has nothing to do with this. Salvation comes from one thing and one thing only, and that's faith and acceptance of Jesus Christ as your savior. *"For by grace you have been saved through faith. And this is not your own doing; it is the gift of God, not a result of works, so that no one may boast" (Eph. 2:8–9).* You can be saved and go to heaven and still be "spiritually dead" here on earth. When love is genuine, you want to be a better person and spread love and kindness in the world. *"Let love be genuine. Abhor what is evil; hold fast to what is good" (Rom. 12:9).* It's impossible to not want to help your fellow man when your love is genuine and you are holding fast to what is good in life.

God instructs us to love ALL our neighbors not just the ones we feel are lovable. Not just the ones that agree with us and share the same political views and religious views as us. He calls us to love everyone even the people that frustrate us, irritate us, annoy us, and that anger us. We are called to love even those that are rude to us, who gossip about us, lie about us, betray us, and wrong us. Jesus said everybody can love people that love them back; that is not sacrificial love. *"If you love those who love you, what credit is that to you? Even sinners love those who love them. And if you do good to those who are good to you, what credit it that to you? Even sinners do that. And if you lend to those whom you expect repayment, what is that credit to you? Even sinners lend to sinners expecting to be repaid in full. But love your enemies, do good to them, and lend to them without expecting to get anything back. Then your reward will be great, and you will be children of the most high, because he is kind to the ungrateful and wicked. Be merciful, just as your father is merciful" (Luke 6:32–36).*

Loving those who are difficult to love is where you begin to love like Jesus. To truly follow Christ, you must love like Jesus loved. Jesus showed love and respect to everyone he encountered. Even when he was being tortured and crucified, Jesus showed love to those who were insulting and mocking him. As he was being crucified, *"Jesus said, 'Father, forgive them, for they do not know what they are doing'" (Luke 23:34).* Only the love that God provides would be sufficient to love our enemies like that. You don't have to agree with somebody or even necessarily like somebody all that much to be kind and respectful to them and show them the love of Jesus through your action and your words toward them and others. *"If anyone says 'I love God' and hates his brother, he is a liar; for he who does not love his brother whom he has seen cannot love God, whom he has not seen" (1 John 4:20).*

We are all sharing the same human experience, and just like you and me, everybody else has bad days too. Everybody goes through trials and difficult times that we know nothing about. We have no idea what someone's struggles are or how their past struggles have shaped them into who they are today. Only God knows all their past traumas and what happens behind a closed door. It is not our job to judge any of God's children. God warns us that if we judge, he will judge us at those same standards. *"Do not judge, and you will not be judged. Do not condemn and you will not be condemned. Forgive and you will be forgiven. Give, and it will be given to you" (Luke 6:37–38).* Our job is to try to show the love of Jesus to every person we meet by how we talk and how we act. Anybody else's behavior and choices are between God and that person and quite frankly none of anybody else's business. Jesus calls us to love and to let God take care of the rest. I don't know about you, but I have enough of my own character flaws and life problems I need help from God cleaning up; I don't have time to be worried about someone else's too. We are so quick to point out where other people fall short and miss the mark, but we struggle to address our own sins and shortcomings. *"Why do you look at the speck of sawdust in your brother's eye and pay no attention to the plank in your own eye? How can you say to your brother, brother, let me take the speck out of your eye, when you yourself fail to see the plank in your own eye? You hypocrite, first take the plank out of your eye, and then you will see clearly to remove the speck from your brother's eye" (Luke 6:41–42).*

We need to focus on ourselves first. Get ourselves right with God first. We need to confess our sins and weaknesses to God and ask for forgiveness. We need to pray for his supernatural presence to lead us and guide us away from continuing to sin. Only Jesus was perfect; the rest of are sinners, plain and simple. We all live in a broken world where sin is all around us and inside us. We all sin, and we all have flaws, and if we want God to overlook our sins and flaws and still love us, we must do the same for others. When Christians flaunt religiosity and cover up their flaws and pretend to be perfect and holier than thou, the world only see us as hypocrites. This is why so many people run away from the church. Christians aren't any less sinners than non-Christians. The only difference really is Christians allow Jesus to pay for their sins on judgment day instead of enduring God's wrath themselves.

It is so refreshing when you do find a church that admits their flaws and confesses their weakness and lets you know you are not alone in your struggle with sin. God knows we are human and aren't capable of always making the right choice. We all struggle. We need to be open and honest and real about our struggles so we can better help those around us that are struggling. God knows the power of sin and temptation, and that is why he lovingly sent Jesus to save us from our sins. *"For God did not send the son into the world to judge the world, but that the world might be saved through him" (John 3:17).* That is a loving father. He isn't the cosmic killjoy that he has been made out to be.

Satan lies and tells you that you aren't good enough and that your sins are too dark and too deep for God's love and forgiveness. This is a deadly trap that keeps so many souls far from God. The truth is God is love, and all he wants is for humans to be loving to each other in all circumstances. He came into this world to save us NOT to judge us. That is the promise that everyone who accepts Jesus can bank on. God loves you, and your sins are forgiven, and you are not judged. Jesus has already spoken for you. You are washed clean. *"As far as the east is from the west, so far has He removed our transgressions from us" (Ps. 103:12).* That is how we love. We don't keep records of the wrongs that are done to us. God told us that love covers a multitude of sins. *"Above all, keep loving one another earnestly, since love covers a multitude of sins" (1 Pet. 4:8).*

We need God to pour his love over us so that it changes our hearts and minds toward other people. When we hurt our fellow man, when we gossip about them, lie to them, steal from them, betray them, backstab them, we are serving Satan, not God. For God said anybody who hates does not know him. God loves all his children, and he made each and every single one of us uniquely special. God knows everything about us, and he loves all your brothers and sisters just as much as he loves you because he is a good, good father. We love, not because it's easy, but because it is the perfect will of God, and it is how we bring God glory. *"We love because he first loved us" (1 John 4:19).*

All the Bad Feelings

L IFE IS REALLY HARD, and we all experience bad feelings. Feelings of fear, anxiety, nervousness, dread, sadness, irritation, frustration, jealousy, envy, and selfishness. The list goes on. None of these feelings are from God. These are all feelings that Satan has brought into our world when he first convinced man to sin and turn away from God. We all face the same struggles when we don't get our peace and joy from God first. Anger and lack of patience for my fellow man have always been the areas I have struggled with most. I lived a good portion of my life in a constant state of annoyance with others.

When I finally recognized this struggle and went to God with it, God began to change me. I had a very open and honest conversation with God, and I asked him to show me the areas of my life I needed to change, and I asked him to have his spirit fill me with goodness so I could overflow that to others. It has been, and still is, a work in progress. Every day, I ask God to give me his power to overcome my own selfish heart and desires. Some days are better than others, but the bad days have gotten fewer and fewer over the years, and I am confident in God's words that he will continue to mold me into the person he made me to be since I am willing to let him. *"I am sure that God who began a good work in you will keep on working in you and carry it on to completion until the day Jesus Christ returns" (Phil. 1:6).*

We don't have to have our lives all figured out before we can come to Jesus for his forgiveness, love, and goodness. God meets us right where we are. Jesus comes to all of us when we are messy sinners. He came to clean us up, not to wait for us to come to him already clean. *"God demonstrated his love for us in this while we were still sinners, Christ died for us" (Rom. 5:8).* Jesus is the only way to get clean from sin. We cannot clean up our lives on our own. We cannot be holy without Jesus. Seeking God and his kingdom is how we overcome the bad in the world. All that is good comes from God, and all that is bad comes from Satan. *"Every good and perfect gift is from above, coming down from the Father" (James 1:17).*

God's spirit is what provides us with all the fruit of life. Our own flesh and desires are what lead us to sin. *"For the flesh desires what is contrary to the spirit, and the spirit what is contrary to the flesh. They are in conflict with each other so you are not to do whatever you want... The acts of the flesh are obvious; sexual immorality, impurity, debauchery, idolatry and witchcraft; hatred, discord, jealousy, fits of rage, selfish ambition, dissensions, orgies and the like... But the fruits of the spirit are love, joy, peace, forbearance, kindness, goodness, faithfulness, gentleness and self-control" (Gal. 5:17–23).* The desires of our flesh are in opposition to the desire of God's spirit. We must actively choose to deny our own fleshly desires and receive with humble hearts God's spirit and his good gifts. *"Those who belong to Christ Jesus have crucified the flesh with its passion and desires" (Gal. 5:24).* It is only through God's Holy Spirit within us that we are able to successfully overcome our own selfish ways.

We are dependent on God to provide us with these good gifts; they do not come naturally to humans. The fruits of the spirit are all beautiful gifts that bring life to your soul. God tells us to seek out this goodness. Look for it all around you. See God's glory in nature, in scripture, in your family and friends, and in the whole world. The Bible instructs us to set our minds on the good in the world and stop focusing on all the bad. *"Finally, brothers, whatever is true, whatever is noble, whatever is right, whatever is pure, whatever is lovely, whatever is admirable—if anything is excellent or praise-worthy—think about such things" (Phil. 4:8).* It's so easy to complain and point out all the bad in life; it takes God to change your heart and mind to flip how you see the world and allow the good to shine through all the bad. When you view the world through the goodness of God, everything changes! You can tolerate what was previously annoying and intolerable to you. You can love those you used to dislike. You can put other's needs and happiness above your own. You can live to serve and help others instead of feeding your own ego and desires. It is God who provides these spiritual gifts, and it is through him that we can overcome ourselves. *"I can do all things through Christ who strengthens me" (Phil. 4:13).*

Our actions and words are very powerful and can have lasting repercussions on not only ourselves but on our fellow man. When any of these feelings arise—fear, anger, frustration, rage, annoyance, or any other negative emotion—before we react and say or do something that we will regret that we can't take back, we must go to God. Seek his wise counsel whenever you feel anything other than peace; ask him to reveal his solution to you. *"But if any of you lacks wisdom, let him ask God, who gives to all generously and without reproach, and it will be given to him" (James 1:5).* Go to God in prayer, and he will show you the path that sets you free from all the bad feelings. *"Be angry, and do not sin. Meditate within your heart on your bed and be still" (Ps. 4:4).* Sadly, many people only come to God when they have hit rock bottom or they have exhausted all their earthly advice, counsel, and help. So much heartbreak and worry could be eliminated if you go to God first instead of last.

"The righteous cry, and the Lord hears and delivers them out of ALL their troubles" (Ps. 34:17; emphasis mine). Notice God doesn't say some troubles; he says all troubles. There is not a single situation that anyone could ever find themselves in that the God of the universe has not already seen or foreseen. Nothing is new to the Lord, and the Lord is never caught off guard or by surprise. He knows all things past, present, and future. There are no earthly circumstances that can't be miraculously fixed by the Creator of the universe, if he so chooses. God wants you to come to him with an honest, open heart when you are struggling with any bad feelings or times of trouble. Only the God of peace can change your heart and mind. Let him fill you with his spirit of love, peace, patience, kind-

ness, self-control and don't allow yourself to respond as you would normally but as Jesus would respond. This practice of self-control and allowing God to control your responses in life and not your emotions to control them is counterintuitive to the human condition. You must actively practice this level of self-control. Going to God first in all areas of your life is the only way to overcome our emotional responses.

"In all your ways, acknowledge him and he will make your path straight" (Prov. 3:6). God will never steer your wrong or cause you regret. All his ways are perfect, and he knows every potential outcome of every situation, and only he knows the best answer or choice. God knows what will defuse a situation and what will escalate a conflict. We must acknowledge God as the all-knowing God that he is and recognize that we are mere humans who quite honestly don't know much of anything even though we think we may. When we submit ourselves under God's authority and allow him to lead us instead of letting our own emotions and feelings guide us, we start to be more like Christ. Jesus always said what was true and right, but he did it with grace. He would call out sin and injustice, but he did it in a nonjudgmental, nonconfrontational manner. He always responded in love first then showed a better way to handle all situations. A way that brought peace and order to the world and not more division and conflict. Jesus told us, *"Blessed are the peacemakers, for they will be called children of God" (Matt. 5:9).*

When you feel fear, Satan is at work in your life. Fear is not from God! Fear is from our enemy Satan! It is his favorite tactic to cause us to doubt God's goodness and power. *"For God did not give us a spirit of fear, but of the Holy Spirit who gives you mighty power and love and self-control" (2 Tim. 1:7).* God says, *"Do not fear, for I am with you; do not be dismayed, for I am your God. I will strengthen you and help you; I will uphold you with my righteous right hand" (Isa. 41:10).* If anything in life is causing you fear or anxiety, present it to God and ask him to reveal his truth to you about that situation. Satan knows your fears, anxieties, and your weaknesses, and he can't wait to use them against you to tempt you to sin or to believe a lie about God or yourself or your salvation.

Worry, fear, and anxiety are the most common feelings Satan plaques humanity with. He loves to cause stress and unsettling feelings inside us and around us. Our truth comes from Jesus though, and Jesus said, *"Therefore I tell you, do not worry about your life, what you will eat or drink or about your body or what you will wear… Can anyone of you by worrying add a single hour to your life? But seek first his kingdom and his righteousness and all these things will be given to you as well. Therefore, do not worry about tomorrow, for tomorrow will worry about itself. Each day has enough trouble of its own"* (Matt. 6:25, 27, 33–34).

Each day has enough trouble of its own; isn't that some truth right there? If worrying won't ever change an outcome, why do us humans spend so much time worrying? Instead, God invites us to *"cast all your anxiety on him because he cares for you" (1 Pet. 5:7)*. Isn't that a beautiful thought? When we are struggling, isn't that what we all desire and need, someone to care for us? Sometimes we are so distraught with the worries of life that it is hard to care for ourselves. The God of the universe is telling you that these weights and burdens we carry are too heavy for us and we were never meant to carry them. Jesus will willingly take them from you and give you peace in return when you go to him and put all your hope, faith, and trust in his goodness. Jesus said, *"Come to me all you who are weary and burdened, and I will give you rest. Take my yoke upon you and learn from me, for I am gentle and humble in heart, and you will find rest for your souls. For my yoke is easy and my burden is light"* (Matt. 11:28–30).

God is so good; he wants to replace all the stress, worry, and anxiety in life with rest for our souls. We can all use rest! This world will run us all into the ground if we don't stop and spend time resting with Jesus. *"Do not be anxious about anything, but in everything by prayer and supplication, with thanksgiving let your request be made known to God and the peace of God, which surpasses all understanding, will guard your hearts and minds in Christ Jesus" (Phil. 4:5–7)*. I can tell you that I have personally seen this promise fulfilled in my own life. A few years back I had a serious trial in my life where it felt like my whole world was crashing down around me and everything that I had worked so hard for was being ripped right out from under me. There was no good way forward that I could see, and the stress, worry, and uncertainty of life seemed too much for me to bear. My emotional and mental state was at an all-time low. I wasted my time searching this world for the help and answers that I so foolishly forgot only God can provide. After several months of saying I was surrendering all my worries to God, only to take them back moments, days, or weeks, later I finally came to a breaking point. I was face down bawling my eyes out to God begging for help. I almost immediately felt his spirit sweep through me, and a warm tingling feeling rise up from deep in my soul and soothe my entire body in the most calm, peaceful, loving way ever. *"The peace that surpasses all understanding" (Phil. 4:7).*

Now this feeling was nothing new to me; I get this frequently when I spend time abiding with God and seeking his will for my life. This time, however, I also felt for the first time what felt like a physical but spiritual hug (the best way I can think to describe it). I could also clearly hear (I use the term hear loosely because it was not audible, but it was as if I heard it in my soul audibly) God telling me everything was going to be just fine and he had it all under control and I didn't need to worry about it anymore; I just had to surrender it to him and trust that he was in control. Instantly, I felt that weight that had felt so unbearably heavy and crushing just seconds early vanish. *Poof!* Gone just like that. It never returned, and God very quickly, within the following days, weeks, and months, revealed his plans to me and worked out all the kinks I had previously felt were impossible. I truly did have a peace that didn't make any sense for the circumstances I was facing. I know people all over the world feel that same sense of hopelessness, fear, stress, anxiety, and depression every day. I hope you find truth in the Word of God that these feelings don't need to plaque you and stop you from experiencing the joy that God wants for you in life. Go to him and he will give you what your soul needs most. Like food and water for your physical body, God's rest is an essential part of your spiritual, emotional and mental well-being. Only God can truly quench the hunger and thirst of your soul.

"Jesus said to her, 'Everyone who drinks of this water will thirst again, but whoever drinks of the water that I will give will never be thirsty again. The water that I will give him will become in him a spring of living water welling up to eternal life'" (John 4:13–14). Living water flowing within in you from God can sustain you in even the most hostile environments and situations. Next time you feel any bad feelings at all, go to God, cast it at the feet of the cross, and let God show you just how powerful, loving, and good he is.

Forgiveness

A**S HE WAS DYING** on the cross for the sins of humanity, *"Jesus said, 'Father, forgive them, for they do not know what they are doing'" (Luke 23:34).* Jesus was loving and faithful to God's work until the end. Again, he showed us perfect obedience to God's will. Jesus knew what many of us don't realize. *"For our struggle is not against flesh and blood, but against the rulers, against the authorities, against the powers of this dark world and against the spiritual forces of evil in the heavenly realms" (Eph. 6:12).* We are slaves to the darkness that Satan has created around us. People everywhere are still captive and slaves to the powers of the spiritual world. We must pray for the evil we see around us, not repay evil for evil. *"Do not repay evil with evil or insult with insult, but be a blessing, because to this you were called so that you may inherit a blessing" (1 Pet. 3:9).*

Resentment and grudge holding are toxic to a person's health and are the exact opposite of what Jesus taught. Jesus taught that we all need God's forgiveness; we are simple humans, and we don't fully understand the eternal consequences of all our actions or do we understand the demonic presence and influence of the spiritual world all around us. Hurt people, hurt people. When we are wronged, Satan convinces us that we are justified in our anger and retaliation or, worse yet, our tendency to take it out on someone smaller or less powerful than ourselves. This misplaced anger is so often spewed all over the youth in the world. This is why we have generation after generation committing the sins of their fathers and continuing legacies that are unhealthy and destructive. We don't have to allow the destructive actions of others to continue to be a ripple effect into the world, causing more hurt and destruction. That is what Satan thrives on. We can call upon God's grace and mercy to remind us that we all have been wronged and have wronged others. God's grace is sufficient for all of us. We don't need others to dictate our reaction to their missteps. God can worry about that. Remember, we are all sinners, and we all fall short of God's perfection and glory. *"For all have sinned and fall short of the glory of God" (Rom. 3:23).*

If you want God to forgive you for all the times you have missed the mark and wronged him, you also must forgive others for when they have wronged you. If you want God to show you mercy, you must extend that mercy to others. *"Be kind to one another, tenderhearted, forgiving one another, as God in Christ forgave you" (Eph. 4:32).* Remember, God loves your fellow brothers and sisters just as much as he loves you. They are his children. He loves them all, and so when you hate your fellow man, you are telling God what he created was not perfect or beautiful. You can't fully love and respect God without fully loving and respecting all that he created. *"Whoever claims to love God yet hates their brother or sister is a liar. For whoever does not love their brother or sister, whom they have seen, cannot love God, whom they have not seen. And he has given us this command: Anyone who loves God must also love their brother and sister" (1 John 4:20–21).*

Forgiveness of others is so important to God that Jesus taught us God would rather you go first and forgive or ask forgiveness and make peace with your fellow man before you go worship him. Jesus said, *"Therefore if you are offering your gift at the altar and there remember that your brother or sister has something against you, leave your gift in front of the altar. First go and be reconciled to them; then come and offer your gift" (Matt. 5:23–24).* God loves all the children he created, even those that don't love him back. He longs for those far from him to repent, change their ways, and come home to him. Most people are familiar with the parable of the parodical son Jesus told.

"There was a man who had two sons. And the younger of them said to his father, 'Father, give me the share of property that is coming to me.' And he divided his property between them. Not many days later, the younger son gathered all he had and took a journey into a far country, and there he squandered his property in reckless living. And when he had spent everything, a severe famine arose in that country, and he began to be in need. So he went and hired himself out to one of the citizens of that country, who sent him into his fields to feed pigs. And he was longing to be fed with the pods that the pigs ate, and no one gave him anything. But when he came to senses, he said, 'How many of my father's hired servants have more than enough bread, but I perish here with hunger! I will arise and go to my father, and I will say to him, "Father, I have sinned against heaven and before you. I am no longer worthy to be called your son. Treat me as one of your hired servants."' And he arose and came to his father. But while he was still a long way off, his father saw him and felt compassion, and ran and embraced him and kissed him. And the son said to him, 'Father, I have sinned against heaven and before you. I am no longer worthy to be called your son.' But the father said to his servants, 'Bring quickly the best robe, and put it on him, and put a ring on his hand, and shoes on his feet. And bring the fattened calf and kill it and let us eat and celebrate. For this my son was dead, and is alive again; he was lost, and is found.' And they began to celebrate. Now his older son was in the field, and as he came and drew near to the house, he heard music and dancing. And he called one of the servants and asked what these things meant. And he said to him, 'Your brother has come, and your father has killed the fattened calf, because he has received him back safe and sound.' But he was angry and refused to go in. His father came out and entreated him, but he answered his father, 'Look, these many years I have served you, and I never disobeyed your command, yet you never gave me a young goat, that I might celebrate with my friends. But when this son of yours came, who has devoured your property with prostitutes, you killed the fattened calf for him!' And he said to him, 'Son, you are always with me, and all that is mine is yours.

It was fitting to celebrate and be glad, for this your brother was dead, and is alive; he was lost, and is found"' (Luke 15:11–32).

This story represents humanity's relationship with God. The younger, irresponsible, greedy son who only cares about himself and the pleasures of this world represents all us sinners out there. The older son represents all the people out there that think they are not sinners (even though they are) because they follow religious laws. As blameless as they may try to be, they are sinners because they do not follow Jesus's teachings that loving thy neighbor is what is most important to God. And that God is the judge of us all, we are not to judge each other. *"Surely there is not a righteous man on earth who does good and NEVER sins" [emphasis mine] (Eccles. 7:20).* The younger son realizes his mistakes and humbles himself before his father and begs for forgiveness. That is what God wants all humans to do. The older son who had been loyal to the father all along was jealous and envious and resentful of the younger son who was welcomed home by the father with open arms. The moral of the story is it's better to turn back to God and ask for forgiveness no matter what you've done than to think you have done nothing wrong and don't need forgiveness. We all fall short, and we all need God's forgiveness. God wants us all to seek forgiveness and repentance for our sins. We should seek out our fellow man who are far from God and try and bring them back home where God is waiting with open arms.

Jesus said, *"I tell you there is more joy in heaven over one sinner who repents than over ninety-nine righteous people who do not need to repent" (Luke 15:7).* Simply admit you messed up and you need God's forgiveness, and he promises he will forgive you. *"If we confess ours sins, he is faithful and just to forgive us our sins and to cleanse us from all unrighteousness" (1 John 8–10).* If it is that easy for God to forgive us of ALL the horrendous sins humanity commits against him, shouldn't it be even easier for us to forgive our fellow man of the offenses they commit against us which in most cases pale in comparison? I understand that there are very wicked, evil people in this world that have committed atrocious acts against humanity who will never seek forgiveness from man or God. Do not worry yourself about such people. Instead, pray for them. *"But I say to you who hear, love your enemies, do good to those who hate you, bless those who curse you, pray for those who abuse you" (Luke 6:27–28).* Ask God to soften their hearts and help them repent and turn from their evil ways and seek his kingdom. If they continue to make the choice to reject God, he will deal with all those people on judgment day. *"Beloved, never avenge yourselves, but leave it to the wrath of God, for it is written, 'vengeance is mine, I will repay says the Lord'" (Rom. 12:19).* God's goal for all humans is not vengeance but repentance.

God tells us to bear with each other and help each other be better. We all need grace and forgiveness. *"Bearing with one another and, if one has a complaint against another, forgiving each other, as the Lord has forgiven you, so you must also forgive" (Col. 3:13).* We are commanded to forgive others if we expect God to forgive us. It is a requirement. Jesus told us, *"For if you forgive others their trespasses, your heavenly Father will also forgive you, but if you do not forgive others their trespasses, neither will your father forgive your trespasses" (Matt. 6:14–15).* Forgiveness is easier said than done. It truly is impossible for man without the help of God's spirit. It can only be done when you allow the Holy Spirit to fill you with God's goodness, love, and fruits. It is crucial to remember that forgiveness is not contingent on an apology or even the offender recognizing they have wronged you. Many times, the people that harm us the most will never admit they have done wrong or that they need to seek forgiveness. Forgiveness is a choice we all have to make on our own accord. When you forgive someone who has wronged you, you aren't just forgiving them, you are setting yourself free as well. You are freeing yourself from resentment, bitterness, rage, and anger. *"Let all bitterness and wrath and anger and clamor and slander be put away from you, along with all malice. Be kind to one another, tenderhearted, forgiving one another, as God in Christ forgave you" (Eph. 4:31–32).*

When you chose to rid yourself of toxic resentment, bitterness, and unforgiveness, you will instantly feel a weight lifted. It is okay to be angry when you are wronged; it is what you do with that anger and how you respond that matters. *"Be angry and DO NOT SIN; do not let the sun go down on your anger and give no opportunity to the devil" [emphasis mine] (Eph. 4:26–27).* Satan loves when we are angry and resentful. He uses our past traumas and hurts and betrayals to keep us in bondage. God never meant for us to carry around all the burdens that others have placed on us. The burdens of this life are too heavy and will weigh us down physically, mentally, and spiritually. Instead, we are to cleanse our souls and forgive and give our burdens to God to carry. Jesus said, *"Come to me all who are weary and burdened and I will give you rest" (Matt. 11:28).*

We must guard our hearts against unforgiveness and know that God is ultimately in charge. He sees all and knows all and will take vengeance one day when he sees fit. We can rest easy knowing that the sins of others are not our burden to carry. God is just and righteous in all his ways, and his perfect will, will be carried out in the end. So until then, we are told, *"If it is possible, as far as it depends on you, live at peace with everyone. Do not take revenge, my dear friends, but leave room for God's wrath, for it is written: 'It is mine to avenge; I will repay,' says the Lord" (Rom. 12:18–19).* Instead, of focusing our minds and energy on holding a grudge, God tells us to do good always to everyone. *"See that no one repays evil for evil, but always seek to do good to one another and to everyone" (1 Thess. 5:15).*

This is the opposite of what our natural earthly response is to being wronged. Again, we must die to ourselves to allow Christ to live inside of us. Kindness and love spread more kindness and love in this world. Following Jesus is counterintuitive to what our broken world is used to. But truly when you love like Jesus and forgive like Jesus forgave you are not only spreading love and kindness in a world that desperately needs it, but you are also being the light of Christ. When you can learn to truly forgive no matter what was done to you, you are defeating Satan. Satan would love to hold all our flaws and sins over our head and to use them to steal our souls from God, their rightful owner. God says that Satan is the accuser of all mankind. *"For the accuser of our brethren, who accuses them before our God day and night, has been cast down" (Rev. 12:10).* Satan tries to dredge up all your past sins and place blame on each of us before God.

I recently heard the amazing testimony of a woman who was betrayed by her husband in the worst way. She was heartbroken, and she was wronged. But because of her faith, she took her betrayal to God and asked hard questions and wanted to understand how she was possibly supposed to do what Jesus tells us to do, forgive. She was deep in prayer and being raw and honest about her hurt to God when she had the most amazing, powerful encounter with God. She was suddenly "taken to heaven." Whether it was a vision or a dream or physically taking place, she did not know. What she did know 100 percent was that she was in heaven and she was standing in front of God, Jesus, and all the heavenly hosts we read of in Scripture (she did not see clear faces but KNEW it was God's holy presence she was in). She explained that she felt like she was in a courtroom-like setting, and she was pleading her case to the heavenly realm about how she was wronged. Then she hears the voice of the most eloquent and well-spoken "lawyer" coming from her right. He was pleading her case for her, only he was doing way better than she could have done. He was using the most persuasive argument, making valid points about how her husband sinned and betrayed her. She turned to see who this was that had come to plead her case for her and realized it was Satan! He was helping her accuse her husband of his sins in front of God. She instantly realized she didn't want to be on the same side of any issue as Satan was and turned away from Satan and her grudge and repented. God immediately forgave her and lifted all the weight of her unforgiveness off her shoulders. God then showed her his great love for her in what she described as the most amazing physical feeling of love wash over her. God showed her not only his love for her but he also showed her his great love for her husband.

This testimony was powerful about forgiveness. Satan is the prosecutor of all mankind. He is in front of God day and night, Scripture says, pleading his case to God about why we all suck and we should be spending eternity with him in hell and not God in heaven. Luckily, if you know Jesus as your personal savior, Jesus is your defense attorney! (Spoiler alert: Jesus wins every case.) Her story was a miraculous, beautiful story that forever changed her life and is a powerful testimony to God as our Father. What Satan meant to use to drag her down and cause turmoil, pain, suffering, scars, and toxic unforgiveness in her life—God used as a powerful opportunity to strengthen her faith and share her story with people everywhere to tell of the glory of God. *"You intended harm to me, but God intended it for good" (Gen. 50:20).*

Her encounter with God not only saved her soul from the burdens of unforgiveness but no doubt that story has also impacted everyone who has heard it as well. God tells us that no sin is too great to forgive. Not yours and not mine and not those who have sinned against us. God loves us all equally. Jesus said we should forgive no matter what; no matter how often we are wronged, we forgive. I want to be clear that forgiving someone and allowing them the space in your life to repeatedly hurt you again and again are not the same thing. If you have any relationship that is toxic and unhealthy in your life, you should cut ties immediately. You can forgive from a distance where you are mentally and physically safe from any abuse. That being said, we should not limit the amount of times that we forgive those who wrong us. *"Then Peter came to Jesus and asked, 'Lord, how many times shall I forgive my brother or sister who sins against me? Up to seven times?' Jesus answered, 'I tell you, not seven times, but seventy-seven times'" (Matt. 18:21–22).*

Now Jesus wasn't giving us an exact number and saying after someone messes up the seventy-eighth time, we can hold a grudge and not forgive (or many translations of the Bible say seventy times seven which would be 490 times). He is simply making a point that we keep forgiving and keep forgiving. I don't know about you, but I for sure will need forgiveness from God more than 490 times! Sadly, that number has been long surpassed. Luckily, God is a God of love and mercy and forgiveness, so I know I am all set because of Jesus's work on the cross. *"The Lord works righteousness and justice for all the oppressed. The Lord is compassionate and gracious, slow to anger, abounding in love. He does not treat us as our sins deserve or repay us according to our iniquities. As far as the east is from the west, so far as he has removed our transgressions from us" (Ps.*

103:1). God says we overcome Satan by doing good to those who have wronged us. Forgiveness is another nail in the coffin to Satan's presence in your life. Satan would love to have hate and resentment festering in your heart because he knows how toxic it is to your soul and to this world. But God says, ***"Do not be overcome by evil, but overcome evil with good" (Rom. 12:21).*** We overcome Satan when we deny our earthly feelings and emotions and put on the spirit of God and his fruits of forgiveness.

We all have done things to others, whether intentional or not, that we long to be forgiven for. Whether the person you wronged accepts your apology or not, know that God does. Sometimes the person we have the hardest time forgiving is ourselves. You must realize that you are a human living in a broken world with fleshly desires that are contrary to the perfect will and desires of your Creator. We all mess up; we all fall short. When you confess your sins to God and ask for his forgiveness, you must believe his promises that you are forgiven, period. God will NOT hold that sin against you any longer. It is totally blotted out of your record. God is not like humans that have a hard time forgetting. Remember true love keeps no records of wrongdoing, and God is true love. He promises that our sins are removed when we confess them. ***"If we confess our sins, he is faithful and just to forgive us our sins and cleanse us from all unrighteousness" (1 John 1:9).***

Do not let your past sins cause regret and scars in your life. That is not what God wants; that is what Satan wants. Satan uses your past sins to constantly make you question your worth and your goodness and even your salvation. God's Word is our truth though, and when he says you are forgiven, you are. ***"Now I rejoice, not that you were made sorry, but that your sorrow led to repentance. For you were made sorry in a godly manner... For Godly sorrow produces repentance leading to salvation, not to be regretted" (2 Cor. 7:9–10).*** Do not allow Satan's lies to keep you harboring shame, guilt, and regret, which will spiritually weigh you down. Leave your sins with God and walk in the truth of God's forgiveness. This is true freedom.

The Power of Prayer

I BELIEVE THAT NEXT to knowing the Word of God, prayer is our next most powerful weapon against Satan. Prayer is simply a conversation with God. Prayer can look a lot of different ways, and a variety of these things should make up a healthy prayer life. Prayer can be done alone or in groups. It can be out load or quietly to yourself and God only. Prayer can be just worshipping God and thanking God for his goodness, or it can be asking something of God. It can be just talking to God like a dad or a best friend. It can be just sitting in silence and trying to hear from God and feel his presence. *"Be still and KNOW that I am God" (Ps. 46:10; emphasis mine).* Spending any time at all where your mind is focused on your Creator is time in prayer.

Our world is so full of distractions, and we bog ourselves down with busy schedules, overcommitting to obligations, and just a, in general, constant rushed, fast-paced life. It takes dedication and mindful planning to spend time in the presence of God and just be still. There is a saying that if the devil can't make you sin, he can at least keep you busy. This is true especially in western cultures. Satan uses our busy schedules to distract us from our walks with God. If you want to have a healthy relationship with God, you must make time in your life for prayer. Prayer is a powerful way to connect with the God of the universe. God allows us full, unrestricted, 24-7 access to him through prayer. God tells us to ask him for anything and everything. God has unlimited resources, and he gives abundantly to those who ask. So ask! God blesses me in abundance, not because he likes me more or I deserve more, but because I ask a lot. I am in pray/ constant communication with God throughout most of my day. I try to follow the words of Scripture and *"pray without ceasing" (1 Thess. 5:17).* Because I spend so much time aligning my life with God's will, he has no problem answering every request I present to him. As I'm sure any parent would do for a child who is grateful and loves them and wants to be helpful and obedient.

God does not always answer my prayers right away, and they are not always the answers I want or expect, but I have full confidence that he hears them, and he knows what's best for me, and he answers them in the way that best aligns with his will for my life, which is undoubtedly more perfect than mine. *"And this is the confidence we have toward him, that if we ask anything, according to his will, he hears us" (1 John 5:14).* If you first align yourself with God's will for your life, there is nothing he won't give to you if you ask. *"If you abide in me, and my words abide in you, ask whatever you wish, and it will be done for you" (John 15:7).* Ask for wisdom, ask for help, ask for guidance, ask for daily needs to be met, ask for protection, ask for peace, ask for health, ask for happiness, ask for the job of your dreams, ask for the spouse of your dreams, ask for blessings and goodness and God will freely give it!

While salvation and eternal life are totally free, paid for by the blood of Jesus Christ, favor with God comes with aligning your life with God's will. *"And whatever we ask we receive from him, because we keep his commandments and do what pleases him" (1 John 3:22).* Keep in mind that God is a good Father and not some magical genie granting wishes, so if our asks are petty and materialistic and selfish, God's answer may be no. *"You ask and do not receive, because you ask wrongly, to spend it on your passions" (James 4:3).* Sometimes God says no because our hearts aren't in the right place when we ask, so our hearts aren't in the right state to receive his good gifts. Sometimes his answer is no because he knows what you think you want but knows what you actually need instead or what would be even better. *"For your Father knows what you need before you ask him" (Matt. 6:8).* Those nos are often only recognized as a blessing much further in life in hindsight. But the more those hindsight realizations or blessings in disguise come up, the more you have faith that one day it will all make sense and that God's plans are always better than man's.

God doesn't leave us to figure life out on our own. He wants you to go to him for help, and he wants to be your provider and guidance counselor. Bring all your requests to him whether large or small. *"Do not be anxious about anything but in EVERY situation, by prayer and petition with thanksgiving present your request to God. And the peace of God which transcends all understanding will guard your hearts and your minds in Christ Jesus" (Phil. 4:6–7; emphasis mine).* Go to God with a joyful heart. Acknowledge and thank him for all he has already done for you. Both what you've asked for and what you haven't but he knew you needed, anyway, and he provided. Then request anything at all and then *"wait for the Lord" (Ps. 27:14).*

This step of waiting is key. Sometimes we must not only wait, but we must also wait patiently for what might seem like a long time. *"Be still before the Lord and wait patiently for him" (Ps. 37:7).* To avoid getting discouraged when you don't see immediate answers to prayer, it is vital you remember that God doesn't work in our man-made constraints of time and space. He is working with unlimited resources in both the supernatural and the natural world. God has no bounds, and even though us humans like to try to put him in a box, we cannot even fathom what all God can do. He works in his time, not ours. *"But do not forget this one thing, dear friends: with the Lord a day is like a thousand years and a thousand years is like one day" (2 Pet. 3:8).*

Some prayers may have a lot of moving parts that all need to realign to make your prayer possible. Sometimes you have to wait. *"The Lord is good to those who wait on him, to the soul who seeks him. It is good that one should wait quietly for salvation from the Lord" (Lam. 3:25–26).* I've had prayers answered in literal seconds, and some have taken years. Some of my prayers are still in the pipeline and God is sorting out all the details, but I have no doubt they will come to pass. God's timing is always perfect because he already knows the ending. God said, *"I am the alpha and the omega, the first and the last, the beginning and the end" (Rev. 22:13).* We must keep faith that God is all-powerful and he does not operate on our understanding. Faith is the key to a strong prayer life. *"And without faith it is impossible to please him, for whoever would draw near to God must believe that he exists and that he rewards those who seek him" (Heb. 11:6).*

If we are to receive the blessings that we pray for, we must believe that he hears us and is capable of answering those prayers. *"Therefore, I tell you, whatever you ask for in prayer, BELIEVE that you have received it, and it will be yours" (Mark 11:24; emphasis mine).* I think God sometimes doesn't answer prayers because he knows that deep down we are doubting his goodness and his power in our hearts. *"Whatever you ask in prayer, you will receive, IF you have FAITH" (Matt. 21:22; emphasis mine).* Many people pray yet don't fully believe in God or his power. They doubt that God can and will do miracles for them if they ask. *"But let him ask in FAITH, with NO DOUBTING, for the one who doubts is like a wave of the sea that is driven and tossed by the wind" (James 1:6; emphasis mine).* Believing in God and his power is key to seeing your prayers fulfilled. Jesus said, *"What is impossible with man is possible with God" (Luke 18:27).*

I have seen too many answered prayers in crazy, miraculous ways to make that mistake myself anymore. I know that when I call to God, he hears me and answers me and gives me the desires of my heart. *"Call to me and I will answer you and I will show you great and unsearchable things you have not known before" (Jer. 33:3).* So all the time I do just that, and God is always faithful to fulfill that promise to me. When you are walking in alignment with God, your desires should align with his will, so it's no surprise he would gladly give whatever you ask. *"Delight yourself in the Lord, and he will give you the desires of your heart. Commit your ways to the Lord; trust in him and he will act" (Ps. 37:4–6).* Although any form of prayer is heard by God, there is something very powerful about group and intercession prayers. When we ban together with other believers and pray, God takes notice. Jesus said *"Truly I tell you that if two of you on earth agree about anything and ask for it, it will be done for you by my Father in heaven. For where two or three gather in my name, there am I with them" (Matt. 18:19–20).* Asking others for prayers and to pray alongside you is a powerful way to strengthen your faith and your community. It also allows others to share in the praise when God comes through with an answered prayer, and it's a way to glorify and testify to his goodness. *"I shall give thanks to you, for you have answered me" (Ps. 118:21).* The more you ask of God and the more you see God answer you and come through for you, the more your faith is solidified.

There will be times in life when the weight of the world feels like it is on your shoulders. The hits keep coming and you feel the walls closing in on all sides and you feel hopeless and full of despair. We all struggle with these dark times, and sometimes the words to pray to God don't come easily because our hearts are so troubled. These are the times that you need to ask God's Holy Spirit within you to step up, take over, and pray to God on your behalf. *"Likewise the spirit helps us in our weakness. For we do not know what to pray for as we ought, but the spirit himself intercedes for us in groanings too deep for words. And the Father who knows all hearts knows what the spirit is saying, for the spirit pleads for us believers in harmony with God's own will" (Rom. 8:26–27).* God's Holy Spirit lives within all believers of Jesus Christ. You have the God of the universe inside your body and mind at all times. When you pray in the spirit, you are allowing God to take over your petition in perfect alignment with his will. *"Praying at all times in the spirit, with all prayer and supplication" (Eph. 6:18).*

Jesus prayed all the time in scripture. He would often go off on his own to be alone in prayer with the Father. This is how we draw on God's strength for our own lives. When asked by his disciples to teach them to pray, Jesus gave us the words to pray to our heavenly Father, *"This is how you should pray: 'Our Father, who are in heaven, hallowed be your name, your kingdom come, your will be done, on earth as it is in heaven. Give us this day our daily bread and forgive us our trespasses as we forgive those who trespass against us and lead us not into temptation but deliver us from evil, Amen'" (Matt. 6:9–13).* When we break down this prayer, Jesus tells us first to acknowledge who God is. ***Our Father in heaven hallow be your name.*** Our heavenly Father is who he is, and his name is holy and should be revered and respected. Then Jesus tells us to seek first the kingdom of God and his will and asks God to help us to be the hands and feet of God's kingdom on earth. We are acknowledging that God's will is perfect and his plan is perfect and that whatever he wants done, we are in agreeance. We want God's glory and goodness to be recognized on this earth just like it is in the heavenly realm. ***YOUR kingdom come; YOUR will be done on earth as it is in heaven.***

We should then acknowledge that God is the one who gives us all things including life and each breath we take. God provides us with all our daily necessities, like food and water. ***Give us this day, our daily bread.*** We then ask God to forgive us and say that we know this means that we must in turn forgive others. ***Forgive us our trespasses as we forgive those who trespass against us.*** Jesus then tells us to ask God to help lead us and guide us on a path that is true to him and not allow Satan to lure us into sin. ***Lead us not into temptation.*** Finally, Jesus tells us to ask for God's blessing and protection against the powers of darkness and all that is not from him. ***Deliver us from evil.*** The battle of good vs. evil is always happening all around us. Not only here on earth but the majority of this battle is being fought in the spiritual realm.

The prayers of God's faithful children are critical in winning these battles in our own lives. ***"The prayer of a righteous person has great power as it is working" (James 5:16).*** When we pray in the spirit and according to God's holy will, we are confident that God will hear, answer, and provide. ***"Let us then with confidence draw near to the throne of grace, that we may receive mercy and find grace and help in times of need" (Heb. 4:16).*** This is our confidence! We have the God of the universe on our side. And as scripture tells us, ***"If God is for us, who could be against us?" (Rom. 8:31).***

We Are Not All the Same

EVERYTHING THAT HAS EVER existed was created by God. *"In the beginning was the word and the word was with God and the word was God. He was in the beginning with God. All things were made through him and without him was not anything made that was made" (James 1:1–3).* All that God created is good and brings him much joy. During each of the six days God created the world and everything in it, he ended each day with this thought, *"God saw that it was good" (Gen. 1:4, 10, 12, 18, 21, 25).* The day God created mankind though, *"God saw that it was VERY good" (Gen. 1:31; emphasis mine).* God made each one of us a beautiful masterpiece for his glory. Think of how creative our God is. If you stop for a second and really contemplate on anything at all, it is amazing to see how brilliant and detail-oriented our Creator is. All of creation screams of his glory and goodness. Think of anything at all that you love. It could be a person, it could be a place, like the beach or a mountaintop or a beautiful waterfall, or it could be a pet. God knew it would bring you joy and pleasure, so he created it specifically for you. You should praise and thank him for that. *"You alone are the Lord. You made the heavens, the heaven of heavens with all their host. The earth and all that is on it, the seas and all that is in them. You give life to all of them" (Neh. 9:6).*

Everything we have ever or will ever experience was created by God. There was a very thoughtful design that went into humanity and all of creation. We are not some cosmic accident or the result of a big bang where everything was created from nothing at all. That theory is pure nonsense, and it is a lie from the enemy. God is our Creator and the creator of all. *"Worthy are you, Our lord and our God, to receive glory and honor and power. For you created ALL things, and because of your will they existed, and were created"* *(Rev. 4:11; emphasis mine).* All Glory and praise for all goodness rightfully belong to the Lord. God is a creative, and he loves variety and uniqueness. One look around at nature and that is plain to see. This can be seen clearly in the variety of flowers, trees, plants, animals, and people that exist. *"For what can be known about God is plain to them, because God has shown them. For his invisible attributes, namely his eternal power and divine nature, have been clearly perceived, ever since the creation of the world, in ALL things that have been made. So they are without excuse"* *(Rom. 1:19–20; emphasis mine).* God tells us that we can clearly see in all creation that there is a creator. There is a brilliant mind behind the design of the universe and everything that exists therein. God is the master craftsman, and we as humanity and the world as we know it are his masterpiece. As much attention to detail as God paid when he created all the beauty in nature, some of it never even seen by human eyes; think how much more he purposefully created you!

"And why worry about your clothing? Look at the lilies of the field and how they grow. They don't work or make their clothing, yet Solomon in all his glory was not dressed as beautifully as they are. And if God cares so wonderfully for the wildflowers that are here today and thrown into the fire tomorrow, he will certainly care for you. Why do you have so little faith?" *(Matt. 6:28–30).* Scripture tells us that God pays attention to detail and he delights in all his work. We are his work. We are all beautifully made to be unique and bring him glory. Every human being that has ever or will ever walk the face of the earth is unique and different. There never has been and there never will be another you. No two people are the same. We all have our own very unique DNA. Even identical twins do not have the same DNA. DNA is God's signature on his masterpiece, you. In fact, God made us all so unique that outside of the well-known differences of fingerprints, many people don't realize that we have many other physical features that are totally unique to

each person as well, including your iris, your ear curves and ridges, your lip print, tongue shape, bumps and ridges, taste buds, your voice, toe print, teeth, retina, and probably more.

Aside from physical features, God has given us all different personalities, talents, spiritual gifts and temperaments. We have different senses of humor and enjoy doing different things. We have different opinions, and we see the world and situations in our own unique way. We all have a different learning style and ability. We all have different challenges and hurdles and obstacles in life. And we are all called to serve God and humanity in different ways. You were a thoughtful creation. You were designed. You are known and loved by your Creator. God tells us he knows each one of us so intimately that *"even the very hairs on your head are numbered" (Luke 12:7).*

God is not distant. He is very close to all of us and is very actively involved in our lives when we invite him in. He knows us each personally and intimately. He knows what we each think, feel, want, and need. Before God created you, he knew what each day of your life would hold. *"Your eyes saw my unformed body. Each day of my life was recorded in your book. Every moment was laid out before a single day had passed. How precious to me are your thoughts, O God, how vast is the sum of them" (Ps. 139:16–17).* His thoughts about you are too vast to count. They are all loving and good thoughts. God's love for you is not a human love; it is unconditional because you are his child. You are not some cosmic accident. God thoughtfully created you. *"I knew you before I formed you in your mother's womb. Before you were born, I set you apart" (Jer. 1:5).* His plans and purposes for your life are beautiful and good. He is proud of the creation that he made, and he created you flawlessly. Your worth is attached to this alone, not to any label humans have ever attached to you. You are his masterpiece, and he loves you. *"He will rejoice over you with gladness, He will quiet you with his love, he will rejoice over you with singing" (Zeph. 3:17).*

Though we are all very different and God made us each to be a unique creation, we all have one thing in common, we all share the same amazing heavenly Father. *"O Lord, you are our Father; we are the clay and you are our potter; we are all the work of your hand" (Isa. 64:8).* And God wants the same thing from each of us, a relationship. God wants each of us to seek him and have our own personal relationship with him. He loves us all and knows each of us intimately. He knows every detail of your life. *"O Lord, you have examined my heart and know everything about me. You know when I sit down or stand up. You know my thoughts even when I'm far away. You see me when I travel and when I rest at home. You know everything I do. You know what I am going to say even before I say it, Lord. You go before me and you follow me. You place your hand of blessing on my head. Such knowledge is too wonderful for me, too great for me to understand" (Ps. 139:1–6).*

Just as we are all very different physically, mentally, and emotionally, we are very different spiritually as well. How God talks to me and guides me and uses me for his kingdom is different than how he talks to you and wants to use you. He gave us all different spiritual gifts as well as physical/mental gifts and talents. Each one of us is an integral part of his plan to rescue humanity from Satan and bring all his children back home to him. God has predestined you for greatness. *"For we are his workmanship, created in Christ Jesus for good works, which God prepared beforehand, that we should walk in them" (Eph. 2:10).* God has an amazing plan and purpose for your life, and he is just waiting for you to seek him out and discover your true purpose and then to walk into it. *"For I know the plans I have for you declares the Lord, plans to prosper you and not to harm you, plans to give you hope and a future" (Jer. 29:11).* God is waiting for you to say yes to him being the center of your life and to allow him to work through you to bring greatness to his kingdom and glory to his name. God wants you to look to him for your purpose and fulfillment in life. *"I cry out to God Most High, to God who will fulfill his purposes for me" (Ps. 57:2).* Remember our lives are to be tools for his plan and purposes, not our own. When we humble ourselves and surrender our will to him, he blesses us. Most times, God gives you something better than you even imagined, hoped for, wanted, or asked for when you are obedient to his calling.

God is complex, and all he created is complex. Neither of which we are fully meant to understand on this side of eternity. All of creation is intimately linked together through our Creator, God. We are all integral parts of the overall universe and God's perfect design thereof. Think of how complex the human body is and how each body system relies on the other for proper functioning. Stop and think of how many thousands of things are happening right now in your own body simultaneously for you to even be alive right now. Your heart is beating on its own, your lungs are exchanging oxygen and carbon dioxide, your blood is flowing and sending fresh oxygen to all your organs, your brain is sending nerve signals to every part of your body, your muscles are moving and functioning, and thousands of other things are taking place. Just as the body is made up of many parts that all have their own very important purposes and functions, they all must work together to function properly, the same is true for God's chosen people, his followers. *"For as one body we have many members, and the members do not all have the same function, so we, though many, are one body in Christ and individually members one of another" (Rom. 12:4–5).*

All the church and all believers in Jesus Christ, regardless of denomination, make up the "body of Christ." *"Now you are the body of Christ and individually members of it" (1 Cor. 12:27).* Although God gives us individual talents and assignments for his kingdom, he needs us to work together to achieve his will. *"I appeal to you brothers, by the name of our Lord Jesus Christ, that all of you agree and that there be no division among you, but that you be united in the sane mind and the same judgment" (1 Cor. 1:10).* A divided church and divided body of Christ is exactly what the Apostle Paul was warning against in this letter to the church in Corinth. Satan has been using "religion" since the beginning of time to pit God's people against each other and cause division and sow discord. It is so sad to think of all the "holy wars" that have existed over time and all the blood that has been shed in the name of God. This is what Satan wants; this is not what God wants. God is brought glory and joy when we show love, unity, and peace. We are not to fight each other over which denomination is more righteous. Remember we all serve the same God, and we all are sinners in need of our great Savior, Jesus. *"There is ONE body and ONE spirit-just as you were called to the ONE hope that belongs to your call—ONE Lord, ONE faith, ONE baptism, ONE God and Father of ALL, who is over ALL and through ALL and in ALL" (Eph. 4:4–6; emphasis mine).*

A divided church is exactly what Satan thrives on. If the body of Christ can't come together and be united, how can we expect to show nonbelievers the way to salvation? We are to unite and spread the gospel together, not further divide God's people. This is where so many "religious" people have gotten it all wrong since the beginning. This is the very reason the religious leaders of Jesus's time rejected him, feared him, and had him put to death. People have a tendency to fight over semantics and lose sight of what it's really all about, love for God and love for others. That is what Jesus taught and preached, and that is our mission as well. We are to be the hands and feet of Jesus Christ to those around us. That is how we are to carry out his will here on earth. We are to represent Jesus in our words and actions to all those God has placed around us in our lives.

"Let YOUR light shine before men, that they may see your good works and they may glorify your father who is in heaven" (Matt. 5:16; emphasis mine). We each have our own light to shine and a job to do to spread the message of the gospel. We are to direct others to the one true God. The talents and gifts God bestows on us for this purpose are limitless. God has unlimited resources and abundance. Nothing is impossible or unachievable for the God who created the universe and everything in it. God can and will use anything or anyone to accomplish his will. God purposely gave us all different gifts and talents because people far from him have different needs and need to be introduced to him in different ways that speak to their circumstances and their heart, which only God truly knows. *"Each of us should use whatever gift you have received to SERVE others, as faithful stewards of God's grace in its various forms, if anyone speaks, they should do so as one who speaks the very words of God. If anyone serves, they should do so with the strength God provides, so that in all things God may be praised through Christ Jesus. To him the glory and power for ever and ever" (1 Pet. 4:10–11; emphasis mine).*

Remember all our gifts and talents come from God, not from ourselves. Whenever we do good, we must humble ourselves to know that it is God's spirit working through us, and he deserves the glory and recognition, not us. Jesus was humble at heart and came to serve not to be served; that is what we are to model. *"For even the Son of Man came not to be served but to serve and give his life as a ransom for many" (Mark 10:45).*

Pride is a deadly sin. Pride is what caused Satan to get banned from heaven for all eternity *(Isa. 14:12–14 and Ezek. 28:12–18).* We must guard our hearts against a spirit of pride which God says brings us disgrace. *"When pride comes, then comes disgrace, but with the humble is wisdom" (Prov. 11:2).* Humility in spirit brings honor to God. *"One's pride will bring him low, but he who is lowly in spirit will obtain honor" (Prov. 29:23).* We are always to point back to God in all situations and allow him to get the credit and glory. Service to others is how we best serve God. *"Do nothing from selfish ambition or conceit but in humility count others more significant than yourselves" (Phil. 2:3).* We are to put other people's needs before our own and count on God to fulfill our own needs. This is God's good and pleasing will for your life.

We are not to question which gifts God gives us and why. We are not to be jealous or envious of the gifts that others have received. God is good to all, and we should never compare our own walk with God to someone else's. To covet is to long or yearn for something or to wish you had something. God commanded us, *"You should not covet your neighbor's house, you shall not covet your neighbor's spouse, or ANYTHING that is your neighbor's" (Exod. 20:17; emphasis mine).* This includes spiritual gifts of others. We should never envy or be jealous of someone else's talents or gifts. We should celebrate each other's gifts and encourage others to step into their spiritual calling from God. *"Therefore encourage one another and build each other up" (1 Thess. 5:11).* Envy and jealousy are traps Satan loves to set for followers of Christ to try and make you stumble along your way. *"But if you have bitter jealousy and selfish ambition in your hearts, do not boast and deny the truth. This is NOT the wisdom that comes down from above, but it is earthly, unspir-*

itual, demonic. For where you have envy and selfish ambition, there you find disorder and every evil practice" (James 3:14–16; emphasis mine).

Pride and jealousy fuel much evil in this world. God says these are demonically influenced thoughts and feelings. All of which are encouraged by our great enemy, Satan. We should never wish we were someone else or wish we had what someone else has. God made us all unique and perfect. *"In his grace, God has given us different gifts for doing certain things well" (Rom. 12:6).* God knows best; he makes the decisions, not us. We must respect and revere him as the all-knowing God that he is and know that he never makes mistakes. He is an intentional God, and everything he does and creates is for a higher purpose. Your talents and gifts were intentional and needed for who God created you to be and who he has brought alongside you to minister to on this side of eternity. If we are to work together to accomplish God's will, we need to lift each other up and speak into each other's spiritual gifts and talents and encourage one another to be bold for Christ.

As a member of Christ's body, you are called to live at peace with others. *"A heart at peace gives life to the body but envy rots the bones" (Prov. 14:30).* Living at peace with all people can be a hard task when you don't abide in Christ daily. Since we are all so different, there are obviously going to be people that you don't mesh well with and that just rub you the wrong way. That is why you need to be rooted in Jesus Christ in order to see others as God sees them and overlook all the flaws we ourselves see in that person. *"If it is possible, as far as it depends on YOU, live at peace with everyone" (Rom. 12:18, emphasis mine).* It may not always be possible to live at peace with all people because of God's gift of free will to all humans and the actions of others, but as scripture says, as far as YOU can help it, live at peace. Simply put don't be the problem, be the solution. The only way to truly be the solution is to put on the spirit of God. *"Abide in me, and I in you. As the branch cannot bear fruit on its own, unless it abides in the vine, neither can you, unless you abide in me" (John 15:4).*

Knowing Jesus is how we "bear fruit"; the spiritual gifts of the Holy Spirit are also called the fruits of the Holy Spirit. *"The fruit of the Spirit is love, joy, peace, forbearance, kindness, goodness, faithfulness, gentleness, and self-control" (Gal. 5:22–23).* When we have Christ at the center of our lives, hearts, and minds, love for others come naturally because it is Jesus within us loving others. A Christ mindset helps us realize that God loves all people just as much as he loves us. Each person is his masterpiece. God is a good Father, and he shows no partiality between his precious children. His love is pure, unconditional, unlimited, and extends to ALL humans. When we view others as a masterpiece of God, it totally opens our eyes up to all the good, beauty, and talents God put in them. This allows us to better appreciate the diverse world God has created and all the different personalities, beliefs, cultures, and opinions that exist. God's spirit helps us to see others as beloved brothers and sisters. If you respect what God has created, you should be able to see past the flaws and see the beauty in any person as God does. The spiritual gifts God gave you are to be used to help bring others to know him. These are gifts to be shared with the world as only you can. If you don't know what your spiritual gifts are, I encourage you to spend some time asking God and really praying that he reveals them to you. *"Now there are varieties of gifts, but the same Spirit; and there are varieties of service, but the same Lord; and there are varieties of activities, but the same God who empowers them all in everyone. To each is given a manifestation of the Spirit for the COMMON GOOD" [emphasis mine] (1 Cor. 12:4–7).*

It's important to understand that what God does is for the common good and for his will and purposes. Whether it makes sense to us or not is irrelevant. We are to not rely on our own understanding but submit our ways to God since he knows best. *"Trust in the Lord with all your heart and lean not on your own understanding. In all your ways acknowledge him and he shall direct your path" (Prov. 3:5–6).* God needs a variety of people to accomplish his will; he needs you! God created us all differently so he could use us for different purposes and to reach different people for his kingdom. *"Now you are the body of Christ and individually members of it.*

And God has appointed in the church first apostles, second prophets, third teachers, then miracles, then gifts of healing, helping, administering, and various kinds of tongues. Are all apostles? Are all prophets? Are all teachers? Do all work miracles? Do all possess gifts of healing? Do all interpret? But earnestly desire higher gifts. And I will show you a still more excellent way" (1 Cor. 12:27–31).

God doesn't give all the gifts of the spirit to every believer. Some people may get only one gift, some may get many, but each person's gifts are unique and personalized. God is so good he will strengthen or reveal your spiritual gifts to you when you ask him to. Remember he said, *"Ask and it shall be given to you, seek and you shall find, knock and the door will be opened. For everyone who asks, receives, and everyone who seeks, finds, and everyone who knocks the door will be opened. Which of you fathers if your son asks for a fish, would give him a snake instead? Or if he asks for an egg, you will give him a scorpion? If you then, even though you are evil, know how to give good gifts to your children, how much more will your father in Heaven give the Holy Spirit to those who ask him!" (Luke 11:9–13)* If earthly fathers can give good gifts to their children, how much more can your heavenly Father provide to those who seek and ask? I already know the answer for my life. I hope you have discovered the answer for yours as well.

Iron Sharpens Iron

GOD CREATED US TO live in close community with others. God knows life on earth is hard, and we need others to walk alongside us and help us through it. God designed us to yearn to be together in community and to live out our faith in our daily activities with other believers. God is brought much joy when we actively spend time in community loving our fellow man. Life is more enjoyable when you spend it with others. Being lonely and feeling isolated is what Satan wants for your life, not what God wants. *"Again, I saw something meaningless under the sun: There was a man alone; he had neither son nor brother. There was no end to his toil, yet his eye were not content with his wealth. "For whom am I toiling: he asked, "and why am I depriving myself of enjoyment?" This too is meaningless—a miserable business! Two are better than one because they have a good return for their labor; if either falls down, one can help the other up. But pity anyone who falls and has no one to help them up. Also, if two lie down together they will keep warm. But how can one stay warm alone? Though one may be overpowered, two can defend themselves. A cord of three strands is not easily broken" (Eccles. 4:7–12).*

God loves when we enjoy time with family and friends, especially if we acknowledge him for that blessing and thank him for fun times and memories with the ones we love. God wants us to be full of love and joy from those around us (as long as we are seeking first to be filled by him and not our fellow man). God wants to be the third strand in Ecclesiastes 4:12 in all relationships. This is especially vital in a marriage. God must be who you turn to in order to be satisfied in life, not your spouse or significant other.

Humans will always let you down because they aren't made to fill you with the love that God fills you with. They simply aren't capable because God didn't create them to replace him in meeting your needs. While God must be the most important part of any relationship, he wants your relationship with friends, family, and all those you encounter to be meaningful and bring enjoyment and joy to your life. God is glorified when we spend time in community serving him, talking about him, studying his Word, and worshipping him together with our Christian brothers and sisters. Our faith can be greatly strengthened by walking alongside other godly men and women who are committed to following Christ and do their best to walk in his ways. Not only can we learn from others from their experiences with God, but we are also better held accountable to stick to our own walk with God when we are spending time with fellow believers. The Bible says, *"As iron sharpens iron so does one man sharpen another" (Prov. 27:17).*

When we walk with other men and women who are leaning into God's calling for their lives, we are better able to recognize our own callings. God will use other believers to speak into your life and spiritual journey and to strengthen your faith. God will bring people around you to encourage you and help you in times of trouble. God wants you to also point out in others the good gifts and talents you see that God has bestowed on them. We should encourage others to step out into their callings. *"Let us think of ways to motivate one another to acts of love and good works. And let us not neglect our meeting together, as some people do, but encourage one another" (Heb. 10:24–25).* We need to motivate and encourage one another to do good as we try and navigate this life together.

Let's face it, life is really hard! And the trials keep coming. I've heard it said before that everyone is either in a storm, just getting out of a storm, or about to go into a storm. Just like an ocean, the waves of life keep coming, and sometimes they knock you down. Although in many ways we are very different, we are all basically the same and are all sharing this human experience. God wants to use our stories to help guide others to himself. We all can relate to having a bad day, getting some bad news, a breakup, a health problem, death of a loved one, loss of a job, financial crisis, or any other millions of different problems you can name. We all feel lost, broken, hurt, confused, alone, scared, anxious, lonely, and sad at times. When we are honest with our struggles with our family and friends, they are able to come alongside us and offer us support and love. When we open up and are real about life's hard moments, we will often find that others are struggling with the exact same situations and also need encouragement that they are not alone in it. *"Therefore, if you have ANY ENCOURAGEMENT from being united with Christ, if ANY comfort from his love, if ANY common sharing in the spirit, if ANY tenderness and compassion, then make my joy complete by being like-minded, having the same love, being one in spirit and of one mind. Do nothing out of selfish ambition or vain conceit. Rather in humility value others above yourselves, not looking out for your own interests but each of you to the interests of others"* (Phil. 2:1–4; emphasis mine).

God is saying, share your stories and your struggles and try to help lift others up and out of their struggles. Share your victories in Christ and how God has turned your struggles into beauty and healing. I've had the privilege of hearing hundreds of people give their personal testimonies of how God has radically shifted and saved their lives. I am blown away every time as I hear story after story of how crazy amazing our God is and how powerfully God shows up for those that love him. I have many of my own stories by this time in my faith journey. The cool thing is I know way more are coming, and every day with Jesus is a new adventure.

Some of the best advice I ever received was from a dear friend who is an amazing God-fearing woman. I was in the middle of what was one of the biggest storms in my life thus far, and my future had never been more uncertain. I had spent months not really trusting God and trying to look to myself and the world to solve a life-altering problem. My path forward was a total mystery to me, and not knowing what may happen was eating me alive for months. Finally, my friend suggested I look at the unknown as an exciting adventure.

She reminded me that I already knew Jesus and had an awesome relationship with God and that he had me totally covered and that whatever happened it would be good because God is good and he only has good plans for my life. She was right, and I am so thankful that God prompted her to speak that into my situation. That was exactly what God knew I needed to hear in order for me to finally surrender all my worries to him. I did, and I was totally at peace after that knowing I could rest safe in his arms and he would handle everything. Literally within days of that advice and me actually following it, God showed up and answered my prayer and very quickly began revealing the path forward.

Sometimes God takes time to fix our problems because he is waiting for us to actually give them to him to solve instead of trying to handle it ourselves. Encouraging words and reminders of truth about who God is and who we are as his beloved children are exactly what we need other Christians friends for. I am so grateful for the Christian friendships God has placed in my life. I truly pray that every person finds friendships as life-giving as the ones God has blessed me with. Getting in a small group is an amazing way to make and build lifelong friendships that will bring joy to your life and help point you to the truth of who God called you to be. We are all here on this planet together, and we need help from our fellow man to navigate this crazy world and help us recognize and avoid all the traps Satan is constantly setting for us. Satan would love to keep you isolated when you have any trials in your life or are experiencing any of life's hardships. Satan would love to convince you that you are all alone and that God isn't with you and can't help you and that no one around you cares. The truth is God sees you in your pain. *"The Lord is close to the brokenhearted and saves those crushed in spirit. The righteous person may have many troubles but the Lord delivers him from them all" (Ps. 34:18–19).*

Have you ever felt crushed in spirit? This is what depression can feel like for many. Feeling like the problems of the world and your own life are just too much to bear. When you feel crushed by the weight of the world, God wants you to know that he is there. God's heart breaks when our hearts break. God sees you and will help you if you turn toward him in your pain instead of away from him. If you harden your heart to God when times get tough, you cannot receive the good gifts he has in store for you. God never leaves you or forsakes you. It is you who has to decide to turn and run to him. He is always running after us in our pain. If you run away in the opposite direction, you will only fall deeper into despair. When you turn and run into his loving arms, he makes all things right in his perfect timing. The good news is that you have the power to make the choice. You could never have run too far from God that he won't meet you right where you are and guide you back to the right path. He promises, *"I am with you always, even until the end of the world" (Matt. 28:20).*

God is the same yesterday, today, and tomorrow, and his promises are always fulfilled. His Word is perfect and 100 percent trustworthy. We should always look to God first for solutions to our problems; he is the great fixer. *"Do not fear, for I am with you; do not be dismayed, for I am your God. I will strengthen you and help you; I will uphold you with my righteous right hand" (Isa. 41:10).* While God is always our first help, he knows we need earthly helpers also. We need other people that can relate to our human experience. We need people to encourage us that things will get better and that this too shall pass. *"For our light and momentary troubles are achieving for us eternal glory that far outweighs them all. So, we fix our eyes not on what is seen. For what is seen is temporary, but what is unseen is eternal" (2 Cor. 4:17–18).*

We will all face very hard things in life, and certain seasons of our lives may be overwhelming and very difficult. It is important to remember that these times are temporary. God puts specific people in our lives for a reason, a season, or a lifetime. God will give you people in your life that can help you discern his will for your life and help you stay on the path that he has called you on. When we are honest and open up to others about our struggles and hurts, God will use people to help you through those tough times. *"A friend loves you all the time and a brother helps in time of troubles" (Prov. 17:17).* We should pray with and pray for other Christians. Prayer for another is a powerful way to walk alongside someone in their time of need and help them lift up their petitions to God.

While God can use our friendships and worldly relationships to help us, we must be careful to guard our hearts and minds from those who are not walking with God. God warns us we must not keep company with those who would cause us to stumble or sin. *"Do not be deceived, bad company ruins good morals" (1 Cor. 15:33).* We all want to liked/loved by others. This is a natural desire that all humans have. "Fitting in" has always been our natural instinct, and we often conform to those around us. It's easy to be pressured into doing something you aren't really comfortable doing in order to not feel left out or ostracized. It is easy to see how we begin to take on the "norm" of our culture and welcome in practices that God has clearly outlined in his Word as not acceptable. The Bible warns about the dangers of "fitting in" and being more concerned about what people think about you than what God thinks about you. The Bible warns, *"Do not be conformed to this world" (Rom. 12:2).* It is crucial that you never allow anyone else's opinions of you to matter more to you than your Creator's. You've heard it said to be careful the company you keep. This is so important in order to maintain your walk with Christ. *"Take care, brothers, that there not be in any one of you an evil, unbelieving heart that falls away from the living God" (Heb. 3:12).* The Bible instructs us, *"Do not be unequally yoked with unbelievers" (2 Cor. 6:14).*

God commands us to love all our fellow man even those that don't know him. God wants our interactions with unbelievers to represent him always. *"Be wise in the way you act toward outsiders; make the most of every opportunity. Let your conversations be always full of grace, seasoned with salt, so that you may know how to answer everyone" (Col. 4:5–6).* God wants us to be loving, respectful, and kind to all people and show them grace. But he wants our conversations seasoned with salt, meaning we are to share the truth of scripture and God's will and not allow false ideology to enter in or keep company with people actively opposing his will. We should always try to bring unbelievers to know Christ and to know truth, but when it's clear they have rejected the message, it's time to cut ties and pray for their salvation. *"And Jesus answered them, 'See that no one leads you astray'" (Matt. 24:4).*

We are living in a society where everyone does what's right in their own eyes again, just like many generations before us that have fallen away from God and his teachings. *"But understand this, that in the last days there will come times of difficulty. For people will be lovers of self, lovers of money, proud, arrogant, abusive, disobedient to their parents, ungrateful, unholy, heartless, unappeasable, slanderous, without self-control, brutal, not loving good, treacherous, reckless, swollen with conceit, lovers of pleasure, rather than lovers of God…avoid such people" (2 Tim. 3:1–5).* We live in a self-obsessed world (think social media and the selfie craze of the world). There is no room to worship God when you worship yourself. We need to climb down off our pedestals and rightly put God back on the throne in our lives.

"Above all else, guard your heart, for everything you do flows from it" (Prov. 4:23). We must be willing to guard our hearts against all this world is throwing at us that goes against the direct Word of God. Again, this is why knowing your Bible is crucial to a Christians walk. Make sure the company you keep does not corrupt your values and morals. *"If we walk in the light, as he is in the light, we have fellowship with one another, and the blood of Jesus, his son, purifies us from all sin" (1 John 1:7).* God calls us to walk in the light and be the light to those around us. God warns us to avoid letting darkness in which will corrupt our souls.

Living a Life of Surrender

ESUS IS OUR PERFECT living example of how to live a life of surrender. Jesus said, *"My food is to do the will of him who sent me and to finish his work" (John 4:34).* That is a powerful testimony! We look at food as a means for survival and sustaining our lives (as well as for pleasure), but Jesus said doing the work of God is what will sustain us! Choosing to do God's will over our own is not easy. Humans, by our sinful nature, are selfish and self-serving. In fact, Jesus says you must die to yourself if you want to follow him. *"If anyone would come to me, let him deny himself and take up the cross daily and follow me" (Luke 9:23).* Living a life of surrender is and should be a sacrifice. We can clearly see that in the crucifixion of Christ. The result of perfect obedience for Jesus was gruesome torture and death. Jesus knew the bigger picture though, and he knew that he needed to demonstrate a perfect life of obedience to show us the way to God. Jesus was scared, rightfully so, but he knew God was with him, and he famously surrendered and said, *"Father, not my will, but yours be done" (Luke 22:42).*

When you surrender fully to God, you relinquish all control to his plans and purposes. *"He who has found his life will lose it, and he who has lost his life for my sake will find it" (Matt. 10:39).* Simply put finding salvation and ETERNAL LIFE in Christ Jesus will make this temporary life as you know it here on earth uncomfortable and unpredictable at times. But your reward will be great one day in heaven. We must put a mindset of eternity at the forefront of our minds, not the temporary pleasures and comforts of this life. Faith in God will sustain us here on earth. Jesus told us that a life following God is hard. He explained that the road that leads to God and eternity is the winding, narrow, bumpy road. The road that leads to destruction is paved, straight, and smooth. He is telling us that doing what is right and just, and following God is not always easy. It is much easier to follow along with the world and all the guilty pleasures it has to offer. That path, however delightful it may look at the time, will lead to death and destruction in the end. *"Enter through the narrow gate. For wide is the gate and broad is the road that leads to destruction, and many enter through it. But small is the gate and narrow the road that leads to life, and only a few find it"* *(Matt. 7:13–14).* Living a life of surrender is a lifelong undertaking. Surrendering our lives to God's work is never done until the day God calls us home. *"Be confident of this. That He who began a good work in you will carry it on to completion, until the day of Christ Jesus" (Phil. 1:6).*

I was recently talking with a few of my best friends, and we were discussing the idea of surrendering your life to Christ. My friend shared that she always pictured surrendering your life to Christ as this dramatic moment: throw yourself face down on the floor and confess your unwavering devotion to God. This made her to feel sort of awkward about the concept. This opened our discussion of what living a surrendered life to Christ means and looks like for each of us. For me, it is a constant moment-by-moment, situation-by-situation, and conversation-by-conversation decision. Anytime I do what I know God wants instead of what I want, I am surrendering my life to Christ. I think living a life of surrender is putting God and others above myself.

When I choose to help someone with something when I really don't want to and I have my own things I'd rather get done, I'm surrendering my life to Christ. When I choose to not say what is on my mind and tell someone exactly what I'm thinking about them or the situation but instead choose to be silent or better yet respond how I know God would want me to respond, I'm surrendering my life to Christ. When I choose to look at the silver lining in a bad situation and thank God for all the good and not complain and grumble about the bad, I am surrendering my life to Christ. When I pick up my Bible and begin to spend time with God in his Word instead of turning on my television or scrolling through my phone, I'm surrendering my life to God. When I choose to not blow up and scream and yell at my kids when they have made another mess or broken another expensive item or are fighting with each other AGAIN but instead respond in love, I am surrendering to Christ. When I have something I just need to point out to my husband that drives me crazy about him but I choose to keep it to myself, I am surrendering my life to Christ. When I listen to that nudge from God to call someone and check in on them, I am surrendering my life to Christ. When I share God's Word with someone even when it's awkward and uncomfortable, I am surrendering my life to Christ.

Right now, as I write this book, I am surrendering my life to Christ. I never wanted to write a book. In fact, I very much dislike writing. I have never enjoyed it. Writing was always my least favorite part of school and college. It's work to me, and quite honestly, I'd rather be doing just about anything other than working. I am writing this book because I believe that is what God is asking of me to do; therefore, I am living a life of surrender. I have felt for years God wanted me to write a book, but I never had any book ideas, and like I said, I didn't want to do it, so I kept brushing it off and thinking that wasn't really what he could possibly be asking of me. I let Satan convince me that I could have nothing valuable to say in a book that would impact God's kingdom in any way. Even as I've been writing this, the enemy has been trying to convince me that this book is a dumb idea and that no one will want to read it or will like it. Luckily, God speaks louder in my life than the enemy does now that I have learned to tune into him more and I can better discern his plans for my life versus my own thoughts and feelings. ***The heart of man plans his way, but the Lord establishes his steps" (Prov. 16:9).***

This book will undoubtedly be exactly what God needs it to be. Even if it changes no one else's life or walk with God but my own. Maybe this book was meant to remind me of all God's wonderous promises and his glorious truths found in the Bible. It may have been his way of asking me to trust him and submit my ways to him. Whatever the outcome, I know that my stepping out in faith is just another slap in Satan's face as I run further and further away from his influence. When I view my calling with an eternal mindset, I know this will all be worth it in the end. I am already seeing how faithfully stepping into the unknown with God is not only exciting but fulfilling. God is revealing more and more truth to me every day about who he is and who I am as his beloved child in Christ. God invites us all to journey through life with him, to learn from him, create with him, to go on an adventure with him, perform miracles in his name, and spread the gospel to the ends of the earth with him. Jesus said, *"Do not lay up for yourselves treasures on earth, where moth and rust destroy and where thieves break in and steal, but lay up for yourselves treasures in heaven, where neither moth nor rust destroy and where thieves don't break in and steal. For where your treasure is, there your heart will be also" (Matt. 6:19–21).*

Don't waste whatever time on this earth God has blessed you with trying to buy, earn, build, and obtain more wealth and earthly possessions. Instead, live for your eternal life and store up in your heart treasures of joy, love, peace, and fellowship with God and your fellow man. Spend your time building up the kingdom of God which is eternal, not your bank account and earthly treasures that you can't take with you when you die. Jesus is our treasure, and we need to store him up in our hearts. Every day in almost every minute, we have the choice to live for our own selfish gain and purposes or for the kingdom of God and his glory. Living for the kingdom of God is where true life is found. Surrendering your life to God is a day-by-day, moment-by-moment choice. The more you begin to make godly choices and follow Jesus, the easier it gets and the clearer the path becomes.

I want to be clear that knowing the right thing to do and always choosing that option are two very different things. I know I do not always live out God's perfect plans for my life in all situations as I should. I fail more often than I succeed sadly. I don't pretend to have it all together. I am very aware of my own sin and shortcomings. But I know that I can turn to God in times of uncertainty, and he will never steer me wrong in how I should proceed. *"I will instruct you and teach you in the way you should go; I will counsel you with my eye upon you" (Ps. 32:8).* I don't always follow God's prompting or live this out anywhere close to perfect, but I try, and I believe that is all God requires of me. God protects me and greatly rewards me when I do step out in faith. *"The Lord makes firm the steps of the one who delights in him. Though he may stumble, he will not fall, for the Lord upholds him with his hand" (Ps. 37:23–24).*

God is faithful to never let me fall, and I am never disappointed when I do choose surrender. God is always faithful to me even when I am unfaithful to him. His plans are always more perfect than mine. I struggled with this for the longest time, and I am still very much a work in process. I am constantly feeling God's Holy Spirit within me, prompting me to share his love with those around me, even perfect strangers. Like I said, many times this is awkward and uncomfortable. Sometimes I will feel the prompt while pumping gas or at the grocery store or at a restaurant or walking down a crowded street. Honestly, for the longest time, I felt a great burden by this, and I even complained to God, "Can't I just pump gas without feeling like I need to evangelize to perfect strangers?" God gets me though, and he is always so faithful and patient with me. He never condemns me when I don't step out in faith, but he greatly rewards me when I do. So being the faithful God that he is, he came up with a solution for me.

I was at a women's event years ago shortly after my complaint, and I heard a pastor read this "love letter" from God over the group. It was the most beautiful letter of scripture conveying the perfect love of God for each of us and his deep desire to be known and loved by us. This letter I now keep in my purse and in my car, and I hand it out regularly to everyone God prompts me to. This letter is a quick, simple thing I can quickly slip into someone's hand or leave in a place they will find. It was a compromise for me to do what God asks of me and him making it less awkward and uncomfortable for me. Many times I just say "This is for you" and walk away before they even open it. Sometimes I'm bold and say, "God told me to give this to you." Either way, I know what God says, *"My word that goes out from my mouth: it will not return to me empty or void but will accomplish what I desire and achieve the purposes for which I sent" (Isa. 55:11).*

God's Word is what changes hearts and minds and saves souls. It's nothing that I can do. God will do all the hard work. My part is easy, just listen and obey. God knows exactly who needs to hear what and when. I should know by now not to question as I have seen countless times how badly people needed to hear these words and how grateful they are that I shared them, but I'm human, and I sometimes allow my comfort to get in the way of my kingdom work. But God is my good Father, and he wants me to be comfortable and not burdened by his work for me. He wants me to delight in sharing the good news. This is the compromise that God came up with for me. God gets his glory, and I don't have to feel like a total weirdo when I'm having a more cowardly day.

Below I've attached this letter, and just like the original writer of it, I encourage you to print it and share it with others. This is an easy practical way that you can share God's Word with anyone. You can leave it for the waiter with your tip. Leave it on the counter in a public restroom, give it to the homeless person on the corner as you slip them some cash, give it to a total stranger you can see is having a bad day, give it to a loved one you know is going through something hard and needs to hear God's great love for them. Watch how God blesses you and brings life to another.

FATHER'S LOVE LETTER
An intimate message from God to you.

My Child,

You may not know me, but I know everything about you. Psalm 139:1 *I know when you sit down and when you rise up.* Psalm 139:2 *I am familiar with all your ways.* Psalm 139:3 *Even the very hairs on your head are numbered.* Matthew 10:29-31 *For you were made in my image.* Genesis 1:27 *In me you live and move and have your being.* Acts 17:28 *For you are my offspring.* Acts 17:28 *I knew you even before you were conceived.* Jeremiah 1:4-5 *I chose you when I planned creation.* Ephesians 1:11-12 *You were not a mistake, for all your days are written in my book.* Psalm 139:15-16 *I determined the exact time of your birth and where you would live.* Acts 17:26 *You are fearfully and wonderfully made.* Psalm 139:14 *I knit you together in your mother's womb.* Psalm 139:13 *And brought you forth on the day you were born.* Psalm 71:6 *I have been misrepresented by those who don't know me.* John 8:41-44 *I am not distant and angry, but am the complete expression of love.* 1 John 4:16 *And it is my desire to lavish my love on you.* 1 John 3:1 *Simply because you are my child and I am your Father.* 1 John 3:1 *I offer you more than your earthly father ever could.* Matthew 7:11 *For I am the perfect father.* Matthew 5:48 *Every good gift that you receive comes from my hand.* James 1:17 *For I am your provider and I meet all your needs.* Matthew 6:31-33 *My plan for your future has always been filled with hope.* Jeremiah 29:11 *Because I love you with an everlasting love.* Jeremiah 31:3 *My thoughts toward you are countless as the sand on the seashore.* Psalm 139:17-18 *And I rejoice over you with singing.* Zephaniah 3:17 *I will never stop doing good to you.* Jeremiah 32:40 *For you are my treasured possession.* Exodus 19:5 *I desire to establish you with all my heart and all my soul.* Jeremiah 32:41 *And I want to show you great and marvelous things.* Jeremiah 33:3 *If you seek me with all your heart, you will find me.* Deuteronomy 4:29 *Delight in me and I will give you the desires of your heart.* Psalm 37:4 *For it is I who gave you those desires.* Philippians 2:13 *I am able to do more for you than you could possibly imagine.* Ephesians 3:20 *For I am your greatest encourager.* 2 Thessalonians 2:16-17 *I am also the Father who comforts you in all your troubles.* 2 Corinthians 1:3-4 *When you are brokenhearted, I am close to you.* Psalm 34:18 *As a shepherd carries a lamb, I have carried you close to my heart.* Isaiah 40:11 *One day I will wipe away every tear from your eyes.* Revelation 21:3-4 *And I'll take away all the pain you have suffered on this earth.* Revelation 21:3-4 *I am your Father, and I love you even as I love my son, Jesus.* John 17:23 *For in Jesus, my love for you is revealed.* John 17:26 *He is the exact representation of my being.* Hebrews 1:3 *He came to demonstrate that I am for you, not against you.* Romans 8:31 *And to tell you that I am not counting your sins.* 2 Corinthians 5:18-19 *Jesus died so that you and I could be reconciled.* 2 Corinthians 5:18-19 *His death was the ultimate expression of my love for you.* 1 John 4:10 *I gave up everything I loved that I might gain your love.* Romans 8:31-32 *If you receive the gift of my son Jesus, you receive me.* 1 John 2:23 *And nothing will ever separate you from my love again.* Romans 8:38-39 *Come home and I'll throw the biggest party heaven has ever seen.* Luke 15:7 *I have always been Father, and will always be Father.* Ephesians 3:14-15 *My question is… Will you be my child?* John 1:12-13 *I am waiting for you.* Luke 15:11-32

Love, Your Dad…
Almighty God

While it may be difficult at times, living a life of surrender should not feel scary or burdensome. Those are Satan's intentions, not God's. God wants us to enjoy serving him and others. For most of us living a life of surrender does not mean having to give up everything we love, donate all our possessions, and move across the world to do full-time missionary work. While God does call many people to do this and the faithful ones that he does call who answer him and go whenever he sends them, I'm sure he has a very special gift awaiting them in heaven, but most of us are not called to make such selfless, drastic changes. God needs people everywhere. God needs men and women in positions and places all over the world. God needs Christians in homes, neighborhoods, schools, and workplaces. God needs Christian men and women as teachers and doctors and stay-at-home moms and dads and plumbers and police officers and cashiers and baristas at Starbucks. You get the point, but God may need you right where you are!

Most people are afraid to surrender their lives to God because they think he's going to ask them to do something really scary and uncomfortable and things that they don't want to do. This keeps many people from fully ever walking into what God calls them to. This fear of change and the unknown is straight from Satan's playbook. He knows that if he can keep us fearing change and fearing the unknown, it'll be so easy to make us not trust God and to step into what he has for us. This is an irrational fear though because God is good. God knows not only what you need in life but also what you want, and he wants to make you happy because you are his precious child.

A pastor I deeply respect, Dave Wilson, always used to say, "Make a dent where you are sent." Basically meaning use your life wherever you may be, in whatever you're doing currently—with your job, your marriage, your parenting, your friendships, your neighborhoods, and schools—and make an impact in those people first. Most people God wants to use right where they are in their current situations. You must be open to letting that happen, and when you do, Jesus will have beautiful plans for your life, none of which will be scary, all of which will be good. Remember God said, ***"For I know*** *the plans I have for you declares the Lord plans to prosper you and not to harm you plans to give you hope and a future" (Jer. 29:11).* His plans are good plans for you. Yes, sometimes God does ask us to do hard things, but more often, he asks us to do easy things that just seem hard because we are scared of the unknown or we don't fully trust him that the outcome is going to be something good and beautiful. God promises that when you seek first to do his will, he will then give you the desires of your heart. *"Seek first the kingdom of God and his righteousness and all these things will be added to you" (Matt. 6:33).*

King Solomon, the wisest, richest man to ever live is a great example of this. God asked him what he would like, and instead of asking for anything material, he asked for wisdom, and God said, "Because you sought first to have wisdom from me, I will give you all these other things." *"The Lord appeared to Solomon during the night in a dream and God said, 'Ask for whatever you want me to give you.' Solomon answered, 'Now, Lord my God, you have made your servant king in place of my father David, but I am only a little child and do not know how to carry out my duties. Your servant is here among the people you have chosen, a great people, too numerous to count or number. So give your servant a discerning heart to govern your people and to distinguish right and wrong.' The Lord was pleased that Soloman had asked for this. So God said to him, 'Since you have asked for this and not for long life or wealth for yourself, nor have you asked for death for your enemies but for discernment in administering justice, I will do what you have asked. I will give you a wise and discerning heart, so that there will never be anyone like you, nor will there ever be. MOREOVER, I will give you what you have not asked for— both wealth and honor—so that in your lifetime you will have no equal among kings'" (1 Kings 3:5–13; emphasis mine).*

Not only was King Solomon the richest king to ever have lived with his abundance of everything both worldly and heavenly, but he was also the most honored and respected king as well. Soloman had great favor with God. That is what God wants to do for all his children who love him. He is a good father and wants to give you good gifts. Every good gift is from him. Surrendering to God is not scary; it is a beautiful, amazing experience.

I once saw a drawing of a little girl holding onto a teddy bear she clearly loved; she was holding it tightly, squeezing it for dear life. In the picture, Jesus is standing in front of her with one hand stretched out, asking for her to give him the teddy bear that she was clearly not wanting to let go of. What she didn't see that the rest of us did was behind Jesus's back in his other hand was an even bigger teddy bear he was waiting to give her. What a beautiful picture! Sometimes we hold on so tightly to things that are bad for us or just aren't helping us in our spiritual journey because they're comfortable and because the unknown is too scary, that we don't have room for what God wants to give us. When this is the case, we end up missing out on something bigger and better that God has for us. God has good plans for your life, and when you trust him and allow him to work through you in any way that he deems necessary, then he bestows his biggest blessings on you yet. Don't be afraid of what God has in store for you, get excited to go on an adventure with him and step into the unknown.

In this global society we live in, it is so easy to bring the message of Christ to people all over the world in millions of different ways. God has a special assignment for you that he knows you'll love and be excellent at! So don't fear what assignment he's going to give you; instead, pray about what you can do for his kingdom and where he needs you to step up your game and shine the light of his glory. *"Let your light shine before men that they may see your good works and may glorify your father who is in heaven" (Matt. 5:16).*

Something very powerful happens in the spiritual realm when we submit our lives to God. You become untouchable by the powers of evil. *"Submit yourselves therefore to God. Resist the devil and he will flee from you" (James 4:7).* God is so good and so faithful that even when we don't step out and do what he calls us to do, he loves us anyway. Remember that it is not by works that we are saved; it is only through our belief in Jesus Christ. It is only because of God's mercy and grace and the sacrificial love of Jesus Christ that any of us are able to stand before him one day righteous in his eyes. It is truly us that misses out when we miss an opportunity to move when God tells us to move. When you trust God and walk by faith and not by sight, that is when he moves the most in your life. You will never have a miraculous moment to share with others and your own personal testimony of God's glory and goodness in your life if you never step out in faith and trust him to do big, unachievable things. You can trust God; he only wants the best for you. *"The Lord is trustworthy in all he promises and faithful in all that he does" (Ps. 145:13).*

Remember that with man, not everything is possible, but with God, all things are possible. The more you trust him to do the unthinkable and unbelievable in your life, the more he shows up and the stronger your faith gets. When you choose to fully follow Christ, get ready for your world to be rocked. We serve an amazing God who does amazing things all the time. We just have to ask for them, pray for them, recognize, acknowledge, and praise God for them. No one does this perfectly all the time, so you have to give yourself grace when you miss an opportunity to step out in faith. God will provide an abundance of opportunities. Every new opportunity is an opportunity to say yes to following God and yes to a life lived of faith.

I relate to what the Apostle Paul wrote to the church in Phillipi, *"I'm not saying that I have this all together, that I have made it. But I am well on my way, reaching out for Christ, who has so wondrously reached out for me. Friends, don't get me wrong; by no means do I count myself an expert in all of this, but I've got my eye on the goal, where God is beckoning us onward to Jesus. I'm off and running, and I'm not turning back" (Phil. 3:12–14).* God doesn't expect any of us to be perfect. We are humans, and he is fully aware of our limitations; remember, he is our Creator. The goal is to continually seek God and his kingdom. Just like Paul, we should all strive to better ourselves everyday by being more like Jesus in our thoughts, words, and actions. *"Let us set aside every weight, and sin which clings so closely, and let us run with endurance the race that is set before us, looking to Jesus, the founder and perfector of our faith, who for the joy that was set before him endured the cross, despising the shame, and is seated at the right hand of the throne of God" (Heb. 12:1–2).*

We should be constantly running after God and following the path that Jesus laid out for us as his path leads to eternal life. As Paul wrote, ***"Do you not know that in a race all the runners run, but only one receives the prize? So run in such a way as to get the prize!" (1 Cor. 9:24).*** Do not just run to run but run to win the prize, eternal life. Don't live for the temporary, live for the eternal.

Raising the Next Godly Generation

GOD LOVES CHILDREN! GOD says that children are the greatest in the kingdom of heaven. *"Whoever takes the lowly position of this child is the greatest in the kingdom of heaven and whoever welcomes one such child in my name, welcomes me" (Matt. 18:4–5).* Children have an awe of the world and an innocence and pureness that brings God much joy. Children are a gift from God, and parenting is an awesome and serious responsibility and great privilege. *"Children are a gift from the Lord; they are a reward from him" (Ps. 127:3).*

While not everyone is called to be a parent, all are called to help raise the next generation to know God. Many people who are not physical or biological parents are still called to be spiritual parents or mentors to the younger generations they get to interact with. This is just as important! It truly does take a village to raise a child. Parenting is hard! Sadly, I would say I've probably had more parenting failures than victories. I've always said that as much as we watch our kids grow up, our kids also watch us grow up. Mental and spiritual maturity is a lifelong process, and we never stop learning and growing. Different people, situations, and encounters help us grow and learn and shape us. We never stop maturing. I do my best to set a good godly example for my children; however, like everyone else, my best is not good enough. That's why besides parenting with my husband, I parent with Jesus. Jesus is always enough!

When I can quiet my life for moments through a crazy, hectic day and be filled with God's goodness and glory, I can shine that light into my parenting. This takes denying my own flesh and putting on the spirit of God. We all want better for our kids than we had. No good parent wants to see their kids hurt or repeating their mistakes. We want our kids to learn from us instead of the hard way. Imparting biblical knowledge and truth in your children from a young age will not only help them find their true identity in Christ but will also help guard them from the lies of the enemy. *"Train up a child in the way he should go; even when he is old he will not depart from it" (Prov. 22:6).*

Teachable moments are what I refer to in my parenting as moments where something happens, usually something less than ideal, where I can use scripture to shine God's wisdom on a bad situation and provide biblical insight into what God would want done in that situation. In these moments, when I can remember to surrender my own feelings and words to the Holy Spirit (I cringe to think of how often I lash out first) are powerful teaching moments. I try to tell my children what it is that God says about the moment, how we should respond, and what God could be trying to teach us through it. If you pray for these moments, God will provide them in abundance. It is our job to raise this next generation to know Jesus Christ. Lest we be like the generation that followed Joshua after the Israelites came to the promised land. *"After that whole generation had been gathered to their ancestors, another whole generation grew up who knew neither the Lord nor what he had done for Israel. Then the Israelites did evil in the eyes of the Lord and served the Baals" (Judg. 2:10–11).*

When entire generations aren't taught scripture, immense evil on this planet is the result. It is our job to teach our children God's Word and his rules. This world will teach your children the rules Satan plays by. This world will expose your child to all sorts of evil things that are not from God and that break God's heart. If you have seen some of the things kids seek these days as "entertainment," you can clearly see what Satan has in store for this generation (think TikTok and social media and all things Hollywood). It is crucial that you arm your children with the truth about what God says so that they are not fooled by the enemy. This world and all the evil forces at work in it will leave your children feeling beaten, broken, and lost if they don't know their true identity as children of the Most High King. Remember, *"Satan comes only to steal, kill, and destroy" (John 10:10).* He is the father of all lies, and his one and only goal is to trip us all up and steal us away from eternal life with Christ, which we are the rightful heirs, thanks to Jesus's sacrifice on the cross. If your children don't know the truth of God's Word like so many men and women, they will fall prey to this world and all the tricks Satan has in store for them. Your children must know that their worth comes from what God says about them, not their peers and this world.

All the false labels that will get thrown at them throughout their lives will only stick if they are not secure in what God says about them. The pressure to conform to this world and fit in will be overpowering if you don't give them the correct weapons to fight back. After God gave Moses the Ten Commandments, he told Moses to instruct all his people to follow his commandments. Moses said, *"These commandments, decrees and laws the Lord your God directed me to teach you to observe in the land that you are crossing the Jordan to possess, so that you, your children and their children after them may fear the Lord your God as long as you live by keeping all his decrees and commands that I give you so that you may enjoy a long life" (Deut. 6:1–2).* Moses goes on to command, *"These commandments that I give to you today are to be on your hearts. Impress them on your children. Talk about them when you sit at home and when you walk along the road, when you lie down and when you get up. Tie them as symbols on your hands and bind them on your foreheads. Write them on the doorframes of your houses and on your gates" (Deut. 6:6–9).*

The more you talk to your children about the Word of God, the more it becomes like second nature for them to apply scripture to their everyday lives and circumstances. This is the best thing you can do for your children. It will not only solidify their faith but also arm them with the arsenal they need to weather any of life's many storms. This world is bringing a whole lot of crazy to our children right now.

The lies of the enemy are everywhere. Only the Word of God makes it clear to see what those lies are. A strong relationship with God is the firm foundation needed to build your life to be able to withstand all the crazy this world will bring you. Jesus said, *"Everyone then who hears these words of mine and does them will be like a wise man who built his house on the rock. And the rain came, and the floods came, and the winds blew and beat on that house, but it did not fall, because it had been founded on rock. And everyone who hears these words of mine and does not do them will be like a foolish man who built his house on the sand. And the rain fell, and the floods came, and the winds blew and beat against the house, and it fell, and the ruin of the house was great"* (Matt. 7:24–27). When you build your life on any foundation other than Jesus Christ, the result will be great ruin whenever a storm arises. Those of us who have lived a while know that the storms of life are constantly brewing. Jesus is our firm foundation, and he is how we are able to escape life's storms unscathed.

I have a full plate at home as many of you do. I work full-time outside the home, and I raise three kids who are active in many sports and extracurricular activities. I also have a home to maintain where the chores feel endless and many other everyday duties I need to fulfill as a productive member of society, but I prioritize time with God and leading my family in faith. If you have time to watch the television, scroll through social media, relax on the couch, take a nap, go shopping, meet friends for a drink, etc., you have time to devote to reading God's Word and sharing it with your children. Teaching your children about God is your God-given duty. There are practical ways to implement this even in our busy schedules. You can share scripture at the dinner table or with your kids in the car on the way to or from school or to and from sports practice. Getting involved in your church and other faith-based youth groups is another great way to show your children the importance of having community to share your faith with. Nightly family prayer time is a wonderful and powerful family activity you can implement to spend time together worshipping God. It is so powerful to have your children hear you pray out loud and to have them learn to pray out loud as well. As we all know, children very closely watch adults, especially their parents, and they mimic us.

Our children naturally long to be like us, and when they see godly role models who love God and wholeheartedly seek after him, it can help shape their identity in Christ and help guide them along their path to walking with Christ. Our family does nightly family prayers. We choose a different family member's bedroom to say prayers in every night at bedtime, and we first start by saying a few tradition prayers like the Our Father, then we ask God to bless everyone in our family by name (including relatives, friends, and pets), then we end with "special prayers." In our special prayers, each person takes a turn thanking God for at least one specific thing (God loves when you praise him for something specific) then anything and everything that person would like to pray about or ask God for help, healing, or blessings with.

It is so amazing to hear your children pray out loud and hear their faith in our heavenly Father! You really learn a lot about what is going on in each other's lives when you know what people are praying about and who they are praying for. Not only can you partner with them by lifting those prayers up to the Father, but you can also see where it is in your family's lives that there may be hurts or struggles where you need to help walk alongside them. This has been one of my favorite things that my family has been doing since our children were young. It is a great way to see how your children are growing and maturing in their faith as well. Our special prayers used to be sweet, fun, and silly to listen to when the kids were younger. For instance, my youngest child loved cereal and would always thank God for cereal and milk. He would also always pray that everyone who was hungry or homeless, God would provide them with enough cereal and milk. As they grow up, their prayers have become more mature. It is so important to make sure kids know that God hears our prayers, and he is faithful in answering them. ***"For where two or three are gathered in my name, there am I among them" (Matt. 18:20).***

God is right there among us when we pray. He hears every word, and the more you ask God for in genuine prayer, the more opportunities he has to answer those prayers and show your children his might, his power, his love, and his care for them. *"If you ask anything in my name, I will do it" (John 14:14). "And whatever you ask in prayer, you will receive, if you have faith" (Matt. 21:22).* Instill in your children that before you go asking God for any and everything and expect him to abundantly provide, you must first have a solid relationship established. *"If you abide in me, and my words in you, ask whatever you wish, and it will be done for you" (John 15:7).* You should always start by praising God and thanking him for all that he has already abundantly provided to you. Second, know that his will is always greater than our own and that which does not align with his will, will not and should not be granted in prayer. *"And this is the confidence that we have toward him, that if we ask anything according to HIS will, he hears us" (1 John 5:14; emphasis mine).* Seeking the will of God should always supersede anything we could possible want or ask for. This is an important concept to make sure children understand. *"But first seek the kingdom of God and his righteousness, and all of these things will be added to you" (Matt. 6:33).* Third, you must fully be surrendered to Jesus to fully receive all the beautiful abundant blessings he has for you. And you must believe wholeheartedly that the God you are praying to is the all-powerful, all-knowing, almighty Lord of all and Creator of the universe with whom nothing that you ask is impossible. *"Therefore, I tell you, whatever you ask in prayer, believe that you have received it, and it will be yours" (Mark 11:24).*

Faith is the key to answered prayers. *"And whatever you ask in prayer, you will receive IF you have faith" (Matt. 21:22; emphasis mine).* God loves to give his children the desires of their hearts. Just as any good parent knows when your children are sweet, helpful, kind, loving, and respectful to you, you are much more likely to gladly give them what they request. When they have been fighting, breaking rules, lying, being sassy, and disrespectful and they ask for something, we are real quick to give a no and feel justified. God, I'm sure, feels the same way; he is much more likely to answer prayers from his children who thank him for what they already have and who spend time abiding in him and knowing him and worshipping him.

"Delight yourself in the Lord, and he will give you the desires of your heart" (Ps. 37:4). It's important to share with your kids your answered prayers so they can see God working in real life and know that his promises are true.

Acknowledge God in front of your children. Tell them stories of how he has done works or miracles in your life. Share about his goodness and blessings in your life. For example, when you see something good, thank God out loud for it. Nature is where I see and feel the Lord's presence and glory the most. Whenever I see a gorgeous sunset or a beautiful waterfall, I acknowledge how great and creative God is and how beautiful he made the world for us to enjoy. *"Oh, give thanks to the Lord. Make known his deeds among the peoples! Talk of his wonderous works! Remember his marvelous works which he has done" (1 Chron. 16:8–9, 12).* Read the Bible with your children. *"Remember his covenant FOREVER, the WORD which he commanded, for a thousand generations" [emphasis mine] (1 Chron. 15).* His covenant and promises are for all generations; it is an *"everlasting covenant" (1 Chron. 17).*

It's imperative that we let the generations behind us know what God says about himself and us. We are to remember his Word forever, and the only way to accomplish that is to instill his Word in the next generation. Take time to explain your faith to your kids and answer questions they have. It's okay to say you don't know the answer. I probably say I don't know more often than I feel like I have an answer for them. Search scripture together for the answers and discuss what you think God would say. But remember, God is a mystery, and we are not meant to know everything and have all the answers. Our minds would literally be blown if we held all the answers to life's questions. God always reveals more when we spend time with him and ask, but on this side of heaven, we will always have questions, and that's okay; it keeps us digging and searching to further know him.

"I love those who love me, and those who seek me find me" (Prov. 8:17). Let your children see you actively seeking God and following in the footsteps of Jesus. We don't need to have all the answers when we can model the actions. Actions always speak loader than

words. God gave parents a great responsibility to model godly behavior to our children and the generations behind us. *"Be shepherds of God's flock that is under your care, watching over them- not because you must, but because you are willing, as God wants you to be; not pursuing dishonest gain, but eager to serve; not lording over those entrusted to you, but being examples to the flock" (1 Pet. 5:2–3).* When we take the time to pour God's love into our children and follow Jesus's example, the heavenly treasures that will result are unlimited as our children go out into the world and spread that love.

"I have no greater joy than to hear that my children are walking in truth" (3 John 1:4). Arming your children with the truth in scripture about who God is and his great love for them is the single most important thing you can do as a parent. Modeling the love of God to them and others is how you set an example that will have a lasting impact. What starts in your home has a ripple effect out into the world. Whether it is a good ripple or a bad one, it will spread. Put on the spirit of God in your parenting to ensure the example you are setting is one that glorifies God and leads them to Christ.

God warns very sternly about steering our children wrong and leading them away from God. *"But whoever causes one of these little ones who believes in me to stumble, it would be better for him to have a heavy millstone hung around his neck and be drowned in the depth of the sea" (Matt. 18:6).* Kind of a scary thought, but that is how important children are to God. Do not lead them astray! Pray for God's guidance and goodness in your parenting and interactions with children. Equip yourself with the truth of scripture so you can be sure how to lead your children and the generations that follow to Jesus. Remember, before they are our children, they are God's children first. God is entrusting us with his precious children. We would be foolish to underestimate the great responsibility that comes with that. Remember, children are actually our fellow brothers and sisters. They are not lesser beings, and sadly, adults get that wrong so much of the time. So much hurt in this world is caused by childhood trauma. Adults underestimate the lasting impact that they have on children. It is crucial that your impact and interactions with children are full of love and not hurt. Hurt children become hurtful adults who spread more hurt in the world. ***"Fathers, do not provoke your children to anger by the way you treat them. Rather, bring them up with the discipline and instruction that comes from the Lord" (Eph. 6:4).***

If you grew up in a home where loving parents were not present and trauma, abuse, and neglect occurred, my heart and the heart of God breaks for you. God is our Father though, and though we have earthly parents, we must understand that they live in this broken world as well. The cycle of abuse can be broken when just one person in the cycle turns their life to God and allows God to turn their brokenness into beauty. God can rewrite any family legacy when just one person decides to break free from Satan. If you are stuck in that cycle, know that it can end with you. It is never too late no matter how old your children are. Jesus is the way to break the cycle.

Trusting God in
Times of Trouble

I F YOU'VE LIVED MORE than a few years, you already know that life can change in a single moment, and certain events in our lives are pivotal moments that can change us forever. It is important that when these life-defining moments arise, which they undoubtedly will, we view everything from a God lens and try to see how even the most tragic and trying moments of our lives can be used for God's will and good purposes. Remember, God does not cause tragedy and unfortunate circumstances, but he may allow them to happen due to every human being having free will. People can choose to love and serve God, or they can choose to reject God and make themselves god and do what's right in their own eyes. The latter choice unfortunately can cause negative consequences not only for the person making the bad decisions but can also negatively impact the lives of others around them as well.

Every choice in life has a ripple effect out into the world around us. Whether good or bad, our choices do affect other people. It is important that when something in your life goes wrong or something tragic happens, you know that God did not cause it, but he will guide you through it if you turn to him. *"I took my troubles to the Lord, I cried out to him and he answered my prayer" (Ps. 120:1).* God is a loving God, and he is there for you, going through it with you, crying with you, mourning with you, and comforting you. *The Lord is close to the brokenhearted and saves those crushed in spirit.* God is waiting for you to come to him in your times of need for comfort, solutions, and help. *"God is our refuge and strength, a very present help in times of trouble" (Ps. 46:1).*

So many people blame God when tragedy strikes. This causes people to withdraw from God and lose faith. We should be running to God in times of trouble, not running from God. God is the only one who can truly help you in desperate times. He is the only one who knows the whole story and the stories of everyone involved. He is the only one who truly knows all sides in any situation and the outcome of the event in the future. We must rely on God's good word and his faithfulness to hold steadfast to our own faith that he will keep his promises to us. *"'For I know the plans I have for you,' declares the Lord. 'Plans to prosper you and not to harm you. Plans to give you hope and a future'" (Jer. 29:11).*

God is a good father, and he has good plans for our lives. When we don't trust God in an area of our life, we are really saying to him that we don't believe that he is good and kind. How insulting, right? I mean when has God ever been unfaithful to his Word? If immediately something popped in your head about a way God didn't answer your prayers or you felt left alone in a painful time or you did feel letdown, I challenge you to think about how you responded to the situation. Be honest with yourself and think whether you truly gave the problem to God and laid your worries and cares at his feet and let him handle it in his own way, in his own time, or did you leave it at his feet temporarily only to come back later and strap it back on your own back and carry that heavy burden all over again 'cause God didn't work quick enough for you? Or did you blame God and harden your heart toward him and run farther from him and into the world searching for help? Did you really give it to God and look to him for help and trust him like scripture tells us to? Did you wait patiently and remember God doesn't work on our time nor does he answer to us? We are on his perfect timing system, not the one made by man. *"I wait for the Lord, my soul waits, and in his word I hope" (Ps. 130:5).*

Did you hope in his Word and his promises that he will be your help? If you did not, it's not too late. When you chose to truly surrender your bad circumstances to God and wait for him to make it good, he will. If the ending isn't good, the ending hasn't unfolded yet. If you wholeheartedly take your problems to God and LEAVE them there, he will turn them into beautiful testimonies of his love and faithfulness. He will not do this in your timing, so get that expectation set real quick. He will do it in his perfect timing. It may be after you are long gone and don't see the fulfillment on this earth, but watch it unfold when you are in heaven with him. God can and will use any event in our life, no matter how small or how large, how great or how tragic, for his glory and to bring others to know him if we allow him too. God doesn't cause our heartaches, but he can use them for his good will. *"Though I walk in the midst of trouble, you revive me, you will stretch out your hand...and your right hand will save me. The Lord will perfect that which concerns me, your mercy, O Lord, endures forever" (Ps. 138:7–8).* Another version says, *"The Lord will vindicate me" (verse 8).*

God knows your concerns and your problems, and he will make it right how he sees fit; he will vindicate you. God can turn any situation around. Satan uses tragedy and heartaches to drag us down and try to get us to doubt the goodness of our God. But no matter what life throws at us, God can use it for good. *"You meant evil against me, but God meant it for good, to bring about that many people should be kept alive, as they are today" (Gen. 50:20).* We serve a BIG God. He can move mountains and make a way where there appears to be no way. Remember when he parted the Red Sea? God can turn any situation around. *"All things work together for the good of those who love God, those who are called according to his good purposes" (Rom. 8:28).*

I like to look at life as a gigantic puzzle. Only God knows the big picture when the puzzle is finished. We only see the other pieces immediately around us that seem to fit together, but we don't understand how it all connects to the rest of the puzzle. Only God knows how each tiny piece all fits together to form his beautiful masterpiece as a whole. One day, it will all make sense when we get to heaven; until then, faith is required.

When tragedy strikes, cling to God for your strength, peace, understanding, and help. ***"Fear not, for I am with you; be not dismayed, for I am your God; I will strengthen you, I will help you, I will uphold you with my righteous right hand" (Isa. 41:10).*** Everyone will have trials and troubles in life. That is a guarantee. Jesus told us, ***"I have said these things to you, that in ME you may have peace. In this world, you WILL have troubles. But take heart; I have overcome the world" (John 16:33; emphasis mine).*** Jesus didn't say you might have trouble, he said you WILL have trouble. He also said we need to look to him for peace, not this world. The peace the world may give you will always be temporary and insufficient. The peace which Jesus gives us is eternal and is unexplainable because it is a supernatural peace. ***"The peace of God, which surpasses all understanding, will guard your hearts and minds in Christ Jesus" (Phil. 4:7).*** The supernatural peace in knowing Jesus cannot be explained, it can only be experienced. It truly does surpass all understanding when God fills you with hope, joy, and peace even in the most trying circumstances.

When you turn your heart and mind to God in all circumstances, he will provide guidance and help. ***"Trust in the Lord with all your heart; and lean not on your own understanding. In all your ways acknowledge him and he will direct your path" (Prov. 3:5–6).*** Do not rely on your own worldly knowledge, which we must admit is extremely limited. Rely on the God who knows all and see all. Remember who has all the power and is in control of all circumstances and allow that truth to be your hope.

This earth is not our eternal home. This is our temporary residence, and it is a broken world, full of hurt and darkness because of our enemy, Satan. While God doesn't cause problems, he certainly doesn't waste a heartache. James tells us, ***"Count it all joy, my brothers, when you are met with various trials, for you know that the testing of your faith produces steadfastness. Let steadfastness have its full effect, that you may be perfect and complete, lacking in nothing" (James 1:2–4).*** When you go through a hard time and look to God for guidance and help and you see for yourself how he shows up in HUGE way and sees you through it, you strengthen your faith.

As humans, we are more trusting when someone has a good track record with us.

I encourage everyone to start a journal of answered prayers or situations God has turned around for you or any area where you asked God for help and saw it come to pass. This will help remind you of God's goodness and power in your life. When God shows up, it is important to acknowledge him and give him Glory. *"And call upon me in the day of trouble; I will deliver you and you shall glorify me" (Ps. 50:15).* The more we see God as a good father and that his heart breaks when our hearts break, the more we run to him in times of trouble, and we don't even question whether or not he has it under control. God is good all the time. Even when we don't see it or feel it, he is working all things together for the good of those who love him. We may never understand how a tragic event had any good come out of it on this side of heaven, but rest assured God will use it for accomplishing his will. Sometimes we must endure hardships for the good of others. It may not make sense or seem fair, but God will be with you through it all. Paul reminds us, *"The Lord said to me, 'My grace is sufficient for you, for my power is made perfect in weakness.' Therefore, I will boast all the more gladly of my weaknesses, so that the power of Christ can rest upon me. For the sake of Christ, then, I am content with weaknesses, insults, hardships, persecutions, and calamities for when I am weak, then I am strong" (2 Cor. 12:8–10).*

In our weakness, the power of God is more apparent. When it is clear to others that things are falling apart all around us yet we still have a sense of peace and calm in the midst of our storms, that is when God's hand is most visible. Jesus is our perfect example of trusting God in times of trouble. Remember, Jesus was not only fully God but he was also fully man. Jesus experienced all the same struggles and problems humans everywhere face and then some. Jesus knew that God's will is always greater than our own and that he is the great I am and all things are under his control and his plan is always perfect.

As Jesus was preparing for betrayal and crucifixion, he prayed to God with full obedience even in the midst of terror, *"Father, if you are willing taking this cup from me; nevertheless NOT MY WILL, BUT YOUR WILL BE DONE" (Luke 22:42; emphasis mine).* Jesus trusted God right up until the end and never lost sight of his earthly mission, to be the living sacrifice so that all could be saved from sin and evil for all eternity. Jesus experienced the full range of human emotions in his last days and was distraught to the point that he even sweat blood. *"Being in anguish, he prayed more earnestly, and his sweat was like drops of blood falling to the ground" (Luke 22:44).* The betrayal, torture, and death Jesus suffered is most likely far greater than most of the trials many of us will face in life. We must look to Jesus's example whenever we face hard times in life. *"We do this by keeping our eyes on Jesus the champion and perfector of our faith. Because of the joy awaiting him, he endured the cross, disregarding its shame. Now he is seated in the place of honor beside God's throne" (Heb. 12:2).*

Jesus had an eternal mindset! Although trying times often test our faith, we are called to persevere and remain faithful. *"My friends, do not be surprised at the terrible troubles which now come to test you. Do not think something strange is happening to you. But be happy that you are sharing in Christ's suffering so that you will be happy and full of joy when Christ comes again in glory" (1 Pet. 4:12–13).* Every one of us will have suffering here on this earth; we can share that with Jesus who suffered and overcame. Our joy should be in knowing that in the midst of our suffering, God is with us and is strengthening us. We've all heard the saying what doesn't kill you makes you stronger. When we allow God to show us through our pain and trials, we come out on the other side of them stronger. Not only can God use troubles to strengthen us, but he can also use them to help and strengthen others who may be going through similar situations.

As Christians, we are called to *"bear one another's burdens, and so fulfill the law of Christ" (Gal. 6:2).* If you know a brother or sister is hurting or struggling, you are called to help them and encourage them in any way God calls you to. You should also offer them up to the Lord in prayer and let them know you are walking alongside them in their times of trouble. If you are struggling, do not suffer in silence. Use the men and women God has strategically put in your life to help you through it. God wants to help shape our character and grow our faith through the events in our life. He wants to use every moment to draw you into a closer relationship with him. *"We rejoice in sufferings, knowing suffering produces endurance, and endurance produces character, and character produces hope, and hope does not put us to shame, because God's love has been poured into our hearts through the Holy Spirit who has been given to us" (Rom. 5:3–5).* He wants you to rely more on his power, his goodness, and his wisdom, not on your own. *"Trust in the Lord with all your heart and lean not on your own understanding. In all your ways acknowledge him and he shall direct your path" (Prov. 3:5–6).*

Remember only God knows the big picture; trust he knows what he is doing. He did in fact create everything we know. All things come from him. *"Everything good comes from God. Every perfect gift is from him" (James 1:17).* He is the alpha and the omega, the beginning and the end, and all things are under his control. Our finite minds can't even begin to understand all that God knows. We are barely scratching the surface of all that is God. *"He has made everything beautiful in its time. He has also set eternity in the human heart; yet no one can fathom what God has done from beginning to end" (Eccles. 3:11).* What we see play out here on earth is only a tiny part of the whole story. We can't even begin to comprehend how what happens here on earth transcends and impacts God's kingdom. *"The Lord is gracious and merciful, slow to anger, and great in loving-kindness. The Lord is good to all, and his mercies are over all his works. Your kingdom is an everlasting kingdom, and your dominion endures throughout all generations" (Ps. 145:8–9, 13).*

Our time on earth is short, but God's kingdom lasts forever. Eternal life is everlasting. Earthly problems pale in comparison to the treasures of eternal life. It is so important to remember that all the pain and suffering in this life are temporary. So when the waves of life come and knock you down and you feel like your world is crumbling around you, remember this promise, one day, *"he will wipe away every tear from their eyes, and death shall be no more, neither shall there be mourning, nor crying, nor pain anymore, for the former things have passed away" (Rev. 21:4).* One day, God will make all things right. The guilty and godless will be punished, and the righteous will reign forever with our King Jesus. All injustice will be dealt with. *"Therefore, we do not lose heart. Though outwardly we are wasting away, yet inwardly we are being renewed day by day. For our light and momentary troubles are achieving for us eternal glory that far outweighs them all. So we fix our eyes not on what is seen, but on what is unseen, since what is seen is temporary, but what is unseen is eternal" (2 Cor. 4:16–18).*

This world and our lives as we know them will come to an end one day. God promises that those who love him will spend all of eternity with him and fellow believers in PERFECT harmony. We must focus our lives on our eternal destiny and ride out the waves of injustice here on earth. We must wait patiently for God's perfect timing. Every situation on earth is temporary, and every bad situation will pass. *"And the God of all grace, who called you to his eternal glory in Christ, after you have suffered a little while, will Himself restore you and make you strong, firm, and steadfast" (1 Pet. 5:10).* Suffering is temporary, and God will restore you when you accept Christ as your Savior. This earth has many troubles, but it is not our final destination. *"We are citizens of heaven, where the Lord Jesus Christ lives. And we are eagerly waiting for him to return as our savior. He will take our weak mortal bodies and change them into glorious bodies like his own, using the same power with which he will bring EVERYTHING under his control" (Phil. 3:20–21; emphasis mine).* This is our promise. Jesus will come back, and one day, everything will be under his control and all wrongs will be righted. Our hope and faith rests in the name above all names, Jesus Christ.

The Spiritual Realm

U NFORTUNATELY, THE UNSEEN SPIRITUAL world is rarely talked about in churches and seems to make many Christians uncomfortable. This is unfortunate because it leaves a lot of our faith unexplained and confusing. When we better understand the spiritual realm, it allows us to make sense of things that were previously unexplainable. There is an entire spiritual realm that is unseen to us humans that greatly influences the seen world we live in. Angels and demons are real. Heavenly hosts are real. All are mentioned in the Bible repeatedly. Long before God created humanity, he created heavenly beings, angels. *"Praise him, all his angels; praise him, all his heavenly hosts… Let them praise the Lord, for at his command they were created, and he established them for ever and ever" (Ps. 148:2, 5).*

In the beginning God created only angels to love and serve him and share in his heavenly realm. Angels are God's loyal servants and messengers that are assigned to help God's children here on earth, to protect them and give them messages and assignments from God himself. *"For he will command his angels concerning you to guard you in all your ways" (Ps. 91:11).* The Bible states that angels are *"all ministering spirits sent forth to minister to those who will inherit salvation" (Heb. 1:14).* God sends angels to minister to those that are to inherit eternal life; they minister to us in many different ways but all under the direction and guidance of God. *"Behold, I send an angel before you to guard you on the way and to bring you to the place I have prepared" (Exod. 23:20).*

Angels are supernatural beings with superhuman power and knowledge. *"Yet even angels, although stronger and more powerful, do not heap abuse on such beings when bringing judgment on them from the Lord" (2 Pet. 2:11).* They are NOT, however, equal to God. They are not all-knowing or all-powerful. They serve God and are under his authority. They are not to be worshipped or elevated above our Creator. Angels are God's helpers, and he sends them to help his children here on earth in need as he sees fit. *"He sent his angel and saved his servants who trusted him" (Dan. 3:28).* God has sent angels to earth to directly help or protect his chosen children.

Peter was freed from prison by an angel the night before he was to go to trial for spreading the word about Jesus's death and resurrection. *"Peter was sleeping between two soldiers bound by two chains and guards stood at the entrance. Suddenly an angel of the Lord appeared, and a light shone in the cell. He struck Peter on the side and woke him up. 'Quick get up!' he said and the chains fell off Peter's wrists. Then the angel said to him, 'Put on your clothes and sandals.' And Peter did so. 'Wrap your cloak around you and follow me.' The angel told him. Peter followed him out of the prison…they passed the first and second guards and came to the iron gate leading to the city. It opened for them by itself, and they went through it. When they had walked the length of one street, suddenly the angel left him" (Acts 12:6–11).*

Angels can appear to us humans as spiritual beings or in human form. Sometimes people know they are interacting with angels; sometimes we are unaware. *"Do not forget to show hospitality to strangers, for by doing so some people have shown hospitality to angels without knowing it" (Heb. 13:2).* Sometimes God sends his angels to meet our spiritual needs, and sometimes they meet our physical needs. God sent his angels to strengthen Jesus in the desert where he fasted forty days and forty nights, *"And he was in the wilderness forty days, tempted by Satan; and with the wild beasts; and the angels ministered unto him" (Mark 1:13).* And before his death while he was praying just before his betrayal and crucifixion, *"And there appeared an angel unto him from heaven, strengthening him" (Luke 22:43).* Angels are fascinating, and they are mentioned hundreds of times in scripture. There are many biblical accounts of angels interacting, ministering, protecting, and helping humans on earth. Outside of biblical accounts, people all over the world claim to have had their own interactions with angels. Jesus believed in angels, so I believe in angels.

While angels are a spiritual force of good in both the seen and unseen realm, demons are also real and very much present in our lives. Demons are the opposing spiritual force of evil in this world. God didn't create demons. God created only angels. Demons were angels that CHOSE to rebel against God and were cast out of heaven before God created humanity. Therefore, God's gift of free will must extend to heavenly beings as well as humans. There is a war going on that is unseen to us that has been going on since the beginning of time. What I am referring to here is the spiritual war that has been going on in the heavenly realm since the fall of Satan. Satan was one of God's angels. The Bible states that Satan was created perfectly by God in the beginning as a holy angel with wisdom and beauty, but pride was his downfall. *"You WERE the seal of perfection, full of wisdom and beauty...you WERE perfect in your ways from the day you were created, UNTIL iniquity was found in you. By the abundance of your trading you became filled with violence within and you sinned. Therefore, I cast you as a profane thing out of the mountain of God...Your heart was lifted up because of your beauty; you corrupted your wisdom for the sake of your splendor; I cast you to the ground"* (Ezek. 28:12–18; emphasis mine). He was jealous and envious and wanted to be above God. *"How you are fallen from heaven, O Lucifer, son of the morning! How you are cut down to the ground, you who weakened the nations. For you have said in your heart: I will ascent into heaven, I will exalt my throne above the stars of God...I will be like the Most High. Yet you shall be brought down to Sheol, to the lowest depths of the pit"* (Isa. 14:12–15).

Satan wanted to be worshipped above God and set up his own kingdom. There were other angels who followed along with Satan, and they were also cast out of heaven down to the earth out of God's presence. Since evil cannot exist in God's holy presence, Satan and all the rebellious angels were removed and cast to the earth. These former angels that choose darkness instead of God's glorious light became demons and have been actively opposing the will of God ever since. The good news we know from scripture is that Satan and all demons have already been defeated by Jesus. While this has not yet unfolded in our earthly realm, it has already happened in the spiritual/heavenly realm. Again remember time and space are not the same on earth as they are in heaven. *"And war broke out in heaven. Michael and his angels fought with the dragon; and the dragon and his angels fought, but they did not prevail, nor was a place found for them in heaven any longer. So the great dragon was cast out, that serpent of old; called the devil and Satan, who deceives the whole world; he was cast to the earth and his angels were cast out with him" (Rev. 12:7–9).*

Satan wants to separate us all from God just like he was. Misery loves company! So he lies to us about who God is and who he created us to be. Satan purposely tries to lie to you and trick you about who you are truly as a child of God. He will do anything to keep you from discovering the truth of God and Jesus and your true identity in Christ. He will relentlessly try and stop you from walking in the plans God has laid out for your life. Satan was banished to the earth where he has set up his kingdom of darkness. Jesus said, *"I saw Satan fall like lightning from heaven" (Luke 10:18).* Since his banishment from heaven, he has been trying to win as many souls away from God as he can because he knows his days are numbered and his reign will end. *"Woe to the inhabitants of the earth and the sea! For the devil has come down to you, having great wrath, because he KNOWS that he has a short time" (Rev. 12:12; emphasis mine).*

Satan is the reason Jesus came to earth. Jesus came to defeat Satan once and for all to allow anyone who believes in him to be saved from eternal separation from God. *"The one who does what is sinful is of the devil, because the devil has been sinning from the beginning. The REASON the son of God appeared was to destroy the devil's work" (1 John 3:8; emphasis mine).* Jesus came to save us from Satan. The Bible very clearly states that the end has already been written and God has already defeated Satan for all eternity, but until that is actually fulfilled in real time, Satan is allowed to wreak havoc on our world by using those who chose to follow him instead of the one true God, the giver of life. Satan has free roam on this earth, and his influence is easy to spot when you are following Christ. *"One day the angels came to present themselves before the Lord, and Satan came with them. The Lord said to Satan, 'Where have you come from?' Satan answered the Lord, 'From roaming the earth, going back and forth on it'" (Job 1:6–7).*

While Satan has TEMPORARY reign over this current world we live in, Jesus reigns for all eternity and his kingdom with have no end. *"Jesus said, 'My kingdom is not of this world...my kingdom is from another place.' 'You are a king then!' said Pilate. Jesus answered, 'You say that I am a king, in fact, the reason I was born and came into the world was to testify to the TRUTH. Everyone on the side of truth listens to me'" (John 18:36–37; emphasis mine).*

God's Word is truth. The Bible was given to man so we could know the truth and not fall prey to Satan and his tricks. Satan is a liar and the deceiver of the whole world. *"The devil...was a murderer from the beginning, not holding to truth, for there is NO TRUTH in him. When he lies, he speaks his native language, for he is a liar and the father of lies" (John 8:44; emphasis mine).* Satan's oldest and most successful trick is to make us doubt God's goodness and then doubt ourselves. Satan makes us doubt our true identity, our worth, our goodness, our callings, and our abilities to live out those callings. When we doubt ourselves, we are less likely to step into what God is calling us to do. When you know the words of scripture, you know the power of God to defend ourselves against Satan's lies for our lives. *"Therefore put on the full armor of God, so that when the day of evil comes, you may be able to stand your ground... Take up the shield of faith, with which you can extinguish all the flaming arrows of the evil one. Take the helmet of salvation and the sword of the spirit, which is the word of God" (Eph. 6:11, 16–17).*

When you are unsure of the outcome but trust God and still step out anyway, that is faith. Faith is how we defend ourselves against Satan. Our layers of protection (our defense) against Satan's trick are our salvation in Christ, which is our helmet, and our faith, which is our shield. God himself will also shield you from all the plans the enemy has for you when you have your faith in him. Our weapon of choice (our offense) is our sword, which is the Word of God! God gave us the weapon we need to defeat Satan; we just need to pick up the sword and fight back! Scripture is our sword. You must pick it up and read it though! We can defeat Satan and rebuke all his lies when we speak the truth of scripture over our own circumstances and over other's circumstances. Shining the spotlight on Satan's deceit causes him to withdrawal. Much like turning on a light causes cockroaches to scatter. Satan is the ultimate cockroach of humanity. We must fight the spiritual forces of evil in a spiritual way.

"For though we live in the world, we do not wage war as the world does. The weapons we fight with are not weapons of the world. On the contrary, they have DIVINE POWER *to demolish strongholds. We demolish arguments and every pretension that sets itself up against the knowledge of God, and we take captive every thought to make it obedient to Christ" (2 Cor. 10:3–5; emphasis mine).* We use God's divine power to fight Satan. Satan knows our weakness and our hangups (our strongholds). He knows where he can get us to slip up and stumble and sin. He knows how to spin our thoughts and turn them into fears, anxieties, anger, unforgiveness. He tries to use these things as strongholds to keep us in bondage and keep us slaves to our sins. We have the divine power to demolish every argument that is contrary to what God says in his Word. Every lie Satan tells you, can be defeated by speaking the truth God says. In order to pull this off though, you must know the Word of God. Whenever you have any negative thought instead of dwelling on the negative, scripture tells us to take that thought captive and make it obedient to Christ. Turn the lies in your head into God's truth. *"His way is perfect: the word of the Lord proves true; he is a shield for all those who take refuge in him" (Ps. 18:30).*

The more you rely on God in impossible situations, the more you see God comes through with a victory and the more your faith is strengthened. The more your faith is strengthened, the larger and larger your shield grows, further blocking Satan's attacks. God will shield you from your enemies, and the more you allow him to, the more you will realize that he won't ever fail you. *"The Lord is faithful and will establish you and guard you against the evil one" (2 Thess. 3:3).* Satan lies and tries to make us think that God can't or won't come through to help us. But we can rest on God's Word to rebuke that lie. All God's promises are true throughout all eternity and extend to all generations. God is faithful, and just like our faith is a shield, God's faithfulness is a shield as well. *"He will cover you with his feathers, and under his wings you will find refuge; his faithfulness will be your shield" (Ps. 91:4).*

Satan is constantly on the offensive. We must remain on guard always and watch for his traps. *"Be self-controlled and alert. Your enemy the devil prowls around like a roaring lion looking for someone to devour. Resist him, standing firm in the faith" (1 Pet. 5:8–9).* He comes to us in all different ways and with all different lies and schemes. God will bless you when you look to him for help when you are under attack by Satan. *"For you bless the righteous O Lord; you cover him with favor as with a shield" (Ps. 5:12).* No matter what destruction Satan is planning for your life, God can flip the script on him. *"As for you, you meant evil against me, but God meant it for good" (Gen. 50:20).* While Satan does have power in this world, our God is infinitely MORE powerful!

Jesus is the way, the truth, and the life. God loved us so much that he sent his only Son to die for us all to defeat the powers of darkness forever. *"For he has rescued us from the dominion of darkness and brought us into the kingdom of the son he loves. In whom we have redemption, the forgiveness of sins" (Col. 1:13–14).* Jesus's death on the cross was not the end; it was only the beginning of Satan's defeat. *"And having disarmed the powers and authorities, he made a public spectacle of them, triumphing over them by the cross" (Col. 2:15).* Jesus is the lamb of God that was sacrificed for us all so that we could be free from the chains that sin binds us with. *"Worthy is the Lamb who was slain, to receive power and wealth and wisdom and might and honor and glory and blessings! And I heard every creature in heaven and on earth and under the earth and in the sea, and all that is in them, saying, 'To him who sits on the throne and to the Lamb be blessing and honor and glory and might forever and ever!'" (Rev. 5:12–13).*

Remember Jesus has already won the eternal battle against Satan. What is done is done. It is written, *"They will wage war against the lamb, but the lamb will triumph over them because he is Lord of lords and king of kings,- and with him will be his called, chosen and faithful followers" (Rev. 17:14).* Jesus broke the chains of sin that Satan tries to entangle us with. Jesus has already set us free. *"So if the son sets you free, you are free indeed" (John 8:36).* Sadly many people don't realize that their chains were broken and Jesus has unlocked the cage. Satan blinds the eye of many to convince them the cage is still locked. It's not friends! Satan only can keep you locked up and bound if you allow him to. Jesus says, "It's open, come out, and walk in true freedom."

While demonic possession of evil spirits is still very much a thing. It is much more common for demonic influence and presence to be prevalent. Many people today are still plagued by demonic forces in their lives. Addiction in any form, severe depression and suicidal thoughts, self-loathing thoughts, feelings of rage, or harm to others can all be examples of areas in our lives where demonic influence is most likely present. Satan uses our fears and weakness as a foothold to enter into our lives and then can create strongholds that hold us down in chains and bondage. Many people are plagued by unclean spirits they have invited into their lives, whether knowingly or not, through their participation in things like mediums, magic, witchcraft, the occult, and the like. God warns us not to mess with the spiritual world. *"Do NOT turn to mediums or necromancers: do NOT seek them out, and so make yourselves unclean by them: I am the Lord your God" (Lev. 19:31; emphasis mine).*

Demons and unclean spirits are very real, and they are present all around us. In fact, one of the most common miracles Jesus performed was the casting out of demons. Jesus also promised his believers that after he died and the Holy Spirit came upon us, we would also be able to cast our demons! *"And these signs will accompany those who believe, in my name they will cast out demons" (Mark 16:17).* All demons, Satan included, know that Jesus Christ is Lord, and they know they are no match for God and his heavenly army. ***"The seventy-two returned with joy saying, 'Lord, even the demons are subject to us in your name'" (Luke 10:17).*** Jesus gave us his authority over the powers of darkness. ***"Behold, I give you the authority to trample on serpents and scorpions, and over ALL the power of the enemy, and nothing shall by any means hurt you" (Luke 10:19; emphasis mine).*** As scary as the thoughts of demons influencing us may be, know that we can break free this and from Satan by putting all our hope and faith in Jesus. ***"Jesus replied, 'Very truly I tell you, everyone who sins is a slave to sin. Now a slave has no permanent place in the family, but a son belongs to it forever. So if the Son sets you free, you will be free indeed'" (John 8:34–36).***

The battle has already been won, but we haven't seen that fully fulfilled yet because God is so gracious and loving that he is giving us more time to win back more souls from the powers of darkness. Remember, he wants to see every single one of his children saved. He wants none to perish but all to come to repentance and have eternal life. It's time to open our own eyes and the eyes of those around us to the spiritual battle underway. Ask God to reveal all the areas in your life Satan is trying to trap and manipulate you. Ask God to give you spiritual eyes to see his truth and spot Satan's lies and influence. ***"You used to live in sin, just like the rest of the world, obeying the devil- the commander of the powers in the unseen world. He is the spirit at work in the hearts of those who refuse to obey God" (Eph. 2:2).*** God warns us that we are not battling against flesh and blood, meaning other humans. We are battling against the souls that are still captive to Satan's lies and deceptions and are blinded to the truth of the gospel. ***"Satan, who is the god of this world, has blinded the minds of those who don't believe. They are unable to see the glorious light of the good news. They don't understand this message about the glory of Christ, who is the exact likeness of God" (2 Cor. 4:4).***

"Bad people" are not our enemy. Satan is! He has tricked many into following himself instead of the one true God. We can use God's Word to fight against this for our fellow brothers and sisters who are still held captive. God tells us, ***"Opponents must be gently*** *instructed, in the hope that God will grant them repentance lead-ing them to a knowledge of truth, and that they will come to their senses and escape from the trap of the devil, who has taken them captive to do his will" (2 Tim. 2:25–26).* That is how we must view all of God's children that are not currently walking in the light of Christ. They are trapped and being held captive by Satan, whether they know it or not. Even though it is obvious to Christians since *"he has delivered us from the domain of darkness and transferred us to the kingdom of his beloved Son" (Col. 1:13).* When someone is under Satan's control, we must be sensitive to the fact that those under his power may not know they are being influenced because they don't know the truth of who God truly is. *"We know that we are from God, and the whole world lies in the power of the evil one" (1 John 5:19).*

Instead of judging and condemning those around us held cap-tive to Satan's evil, we should pray for God *"to open their eyes and turn them from darkness to light, and from the power of Satan to God, so they may receive forgiveness of sins and a place among those who are sanctified by faith in Christ" (Acts 26:18).* Since we are in a spiritual battle for the souls of God's lost children, we must fight in a spiritual way in prayer. We must petition our Father to ban Satan from the hearts and minds of our fellow man. Many people who still don't know God think they are good people and are trying to do good things. Satan disguises his lies to appeal to people and make them think they are "doing the right thing." The Bible warns us that Satan will try and trick us into sin. *"And no wonder, for even Satan disguises himself as an angel of light" (2 Cor. 11:14).* We must ask God to lift the veil that is blinding so many to the truth. *"Beloved, do not believe every spirit, but test the spirits to see whether they are from God, for many false prophets have gone out into the world. By this you will know the spirit of God: every spirit that confesses that Jesus Christ has come in the flesh IS from God, and every spirit that does not confess Jesus is NOT from God. This is the spirit of the antichrist, which you heard was coming and now is in the world already" (1 John 4:1–3; emphasis mine).*

We must pray against the spiritual forces of darkness in this world and point out all the darkness that is disguising itself as light. We must pray constantly for the goodness of God to reach those still living in darkness. The Bible tells us to *"rejoice always, pray without ceasing, give thanks in all circumstances; for this is the will of God in Christ Jesus for you" (1 Thess. 5:16–17).* When you fully trust in the Lord with all your heart and lean not on your own understanding, it is much easier to give thanks in all circumstances. *"We know that in all things God works for the good of those who love him and have been called according to his purpose" (Rom. 8:28).*

God has a plan for each and every human he has ever created. It is our choice to walk with God and discover that plan and walk in his purpose or to walk away from God and turn to the things of this world and the lies of Satan. This is a choice that not many realize the eternal consequences of. God is the giver of life and every good gift. *"Every good thing given and every perfect gift is from above, coming down from the Father of lights" (James 1:17).* Satan is the father of deception and comes only to ruin and destroy what God has created. Jesus said, *"The thief comes only to steal, kill and destroy. I have come that you may have life and have it to the fullest" (John 10:10).* Satan knows when you begin to seek God, and he will do everything in his power to stop you and make you stumble. You must know the Word of God to help you recognize the lies of Satan and guard yourself against them. Satan is not all-powerful like our God! Never give him more credit than he is due. If you don't want Satan ruining your life, tell him! You have the authority to banish Satan from your life. *"Submit yourselves therefore to God, resist the devil, and he will flee from you" (James 4:7).* It's truly that easy. Admit Jesus is your Lord and Savior, ask God to forgive you for your past sins, and tell Satan he can't have your soul and he will flee from you. You have the power to stop his darkness in your life.

"I am convinced nothing can ever separate us from God's love. Neither death nor life, neither angels nor demons. Neither our fears for today nor our worries about tomorrow- not even the power of hell can separate us from God's love. No power in the sky above or in the earth below-indeed, nothing in all creation will

ever be able to separate us from the love of God that is revealed in Christ Jesus our Lord" (Rom. 8:38–39; emphasis mine). God's love is stronger than any force of darkness and evil. When you are saved by Jesus, you are safe from Satan. Rebuke Satan every time you see his presence in the world. God will strengthen you and help you along the way. The more you walk with God and the deeper your relationship grows, the less and less Satan will come for you. But when he does, you will be better equipped to immediately recognize his tricks. Learn to quickly call out his darkness when you see it, rebuke it, shut him down, and tell him to back off! He will flee, like the cockroach he is!

Our Choices Have Eternal Consequences

T HIS PART IS UNCOMFORTABLE and can cause people to shut
down and tune out. I can't stress the importance of eternity
enough though, so please stay with me. This book would
not be complete or accurate without this part since God speaks a lot
in scripture about consequences. Most people live for the here and
now, but we are called to live for eternity. *"He has made everything
beautiful in its time. He has also set eternity in the human heart;
yet no one can fathom what God has done from beginning to end"
(Eccles. 3:11).* Even though God put eternity in our hearts, we can't
possibly grasp what all eternity encompasses or what it will look like.
The mere concept is too complex and too great for humans to understand. This life here on earth is very short, but the next one will last
for all eternity. *"The world and its desires pass away, but whoever
does the will of God lives forever" (1 John 2:17).*

Eternity is such a hard concept for our tiny, finite minds to even
comprehend. It is permanent, everlasting, and there is no end ever
to eternity. Your belief in Jesus determines your eternal destination. I
hope the magnitude of that statement sinks in. There are real, eternal
consequences for denying the Son of God. The wrath of God is real
and is justified. Because God is such a loving, holy God, he cannot
and will not allow sin to go unchecked forever. *"For you are not a
God who delights in wickedness; evil may not dwell with you" (Ps.
5:4).* We saw this with the great flood of Noah's time when humanity

was at an all-time low and the depravity was too much for God to bear. Scripture tells us we will see God's wrath again when the end of earth as we know it comes. *"Be assured, an evil person will not go unpunished" (Prov. 11:21).*

We all sin, and God is gracious to forgive us when we know Jesus as our personal savior, but true evil will be dealt with, and there is no place for evil in the presence of God. *"Woe to those who call evil good and good evil, who put darkness for light and light for darkness, who put biter for sweet and sweet for biter" (Isa. 5:20).* God commands us to *"abstain from every form of evil" (1 Thess. 5:22).* God tells us what is evil in his sight. This is not a guessing game as to what makes him happy and what disgusts him. Again, you must know scripture if you are to know what God expects of you. *"There are six things that the Lord hates, seven that are an abomination to him; haughty eyes, a lying tongue, and hands that shed innocent blood, a heart that devises wicked plans, feet that make haste to run to evil, a false witness who breathes out lies, and one who sows discord among brothers" (Prov. 6:16–19).* If we chose to ignore God's words and warning, the price to pay will be steep.

God has given us all an unknown amount of time on this earth to choose to be in his eternal family or to be separated from him and all his goodness forever. Whether you believe it or not, it is because of the will of God that you exist. You owe God praise and worship for every breath in your lungs and every beat of your heart. You are simply alive right now because God wills you to be, and when he decides he's ready to take your life, he will. Anywhere, anytime, be any means. You and I have zero say in the matter. The only guarantee we all have in this life is that it will someday end. God determines when and how that will be. Your job is to make sure that your soul is ready for when that day comes. Once it comes, you won't have a chance for a redo. You must decide right now if you will accept the free gift of salvation and accept Jesus as your savior and spend eternal life in heaven with God or if you will reject Jesus and spend all of eternity in hell apart from any of God's presence and goodness. Hell is real, and it is terrifying (hell is also referred to as Sheol, Hades, and the pit in the Bible for reference), and scripture talks about it many times. Hell is not our focus here though because I want our focus to be on the good news, which is ending up in heaven or hell is YOUR choice.

Once you have decided to accept Jesus as your savior, you have chosen heaven! You should no longer fear death or worry about when or how you will leave this earth. In fact, I have even begun to look forward to it! Not in a suicidal type of way; I love life! I have a wonderful, beautiful life that even though it gets messy and hard at times, I know God is present all around me all the time. I can see his goodness in all people and all things. I look forward to it because God promises us eternal life in heaven with him. He promises that only beautiful, lovely things await those who love him. One day, when this world as we know it ends or death comes, all the bad feelings will pass away with it. No more sadness, no fear, no worry, no sin, no death, no sickness, no pain, no trauma, no bad feelings. Only pure love, joy, peace, goodness, and happiness await those that accept Jesus. *"But as it is written, what no eye has seen, no ear has heard, and no human heart has conceived, God prepared those things for those who love him"* *(1 Cor. 2:9).*

Heaven is so wonderous that our minds can't even begin to comprehend or imagine how spectacular it will be. When we know we have eternal salvation and we know we are going to God's perfect and beautiful heaven that humans haven't destroyed and corrupted yet, why would anyone have fear or anxiety about death? It's because we fear the unknown. This is a normal but learned human emotion. We need to look to God's Word and his truth to unlearn this behavior. God said, *"The Lord himself goes before you and will be with you: he will never leave you nor forsake you. Do not be afraid: do not be discouraged"* *(Deut. 31:8).* God never leaves us, and when we have him in our lives, we never have anything to fear, not even death. Death is not separation from God when Jesus is your savior. Death is just the beginning of everlasting life with the loving God of the universe. On the other hand, death is eternal separation from God when you don't accept Jesus. This is a hard pill for most to swallow. While this is the choice that some choose and God simply allows that choice, this is NOT God's will. God loves us all, and his goal is to see everyone come to accept Jesus and inherit eternal life. *"The Lord is not slow in keeping his promises as some understand slowness. Instead, he is patient with you, not wanting anyone to perish, but everyone to come to repentance" (2 Pet. 3:9).*

God wants us all to choose heaven. But it is a choice he allows us each to make ourselves. While the Bible makes this choice crystal clear, sadly many people will never read the Bible, so God needs men and women on earth to help make this choice clear to all his children and explain how serious this choice is and the consequences thereof. You are an integral part of the team. We all know people that are far from Jesus and currently have not accepted his free gift of salvation. It is no mistake that you are reading this book right now. It is written for you. God is calling you. He needs you to help build his eternal kingdom and bring his children, your brothers and sisters, home. God is commissioning each of us to *"go into the world and preach the gospel to all creation" (Mark 16:15).* Jesus is the gospel. Jesus is who saves us all from hell. Jesus is our ticket to eternal life. Remember salvation and eternal life are found in one person and one person alone, Jesus. Jesus said, *"I give eternal life, and they shall never perish; no one will snatch them out of my hand. My father, who has given them to me, is greater than all; no one can snatch them out of my father's hand. I and the father, are one" (John 10:28–30).*

When you live with eternity in mind, you should want to help draw everyone you know into an eternity with God. Those of you who know me, know I love a good party! I am definitely a "the more the merrier" type of lady. I don't want eternal separation from anyone on this planet that I have met. I want everyone I know to be at the party in heaven one day. That mindset is what motivates me to go out and tell as many people as I can about the saving grace of Jesus Christ. God wants to use you to do the same. You know people far from God, and you may be the only person they will every meet that may give them this free invitation to eternal life and God's heavenly party. God gave you specific talents and a unique opportunity to attract, interact, and journey through life with certain people specifically so you could tell them about him. It is no accident who God has placed in your life as either family members, coworkers, neighbors, or even random strangers like the man next to you on the airplane or the woman in front of you at the grocery store. Divine appointments happen all day every day. God just needs you to be listening and willing to move on the prompts he gives you. ***"Each person should live as a believer in whatever situation the Lord has assigned to them" (1 Cor. 7:17).***

I hope as you are reading this, God places on your heart the name of someone in your life he wants you to go after and tell about his great love and mercy for them. Trust me, I know this is easier said than done and it often feels awkward, but you have no idea what God knows. He knows exactly what everyone needs to hear and when they need to hear it. What may seem silly or crazy and doesn't make sense to you could be exactly the answer to what the person you are speaking into needed or even prayed to God for. God has already gifted you to reach others for his kingdom. It's time to use those gifts to show others the truth and promise of eternal life found only through Jesus Christ. God is asking you to not only join the heavenly party but to bring as many with you as you can, anyone who will accept the invitation. It's time to get off the sidelines and step into your calling, to go to the ends of the earth and make disciples of all nations.

Because God is such a good Father, we are given many chances to come to him and accept him and receive the free gift of salvation. God loves all his creation, and he wants all to be saved. That's why he sent Jesus to die for us. God gives every single one of us the choice to accept his Word, his love, his forgiveness, and eternal life in knowing Jesus. This is why Jesus said the world would not end until the good news of the gospel was shared everywhere. ***"And the gospel of the kingdom shall be preached in all the world as a witness to all nations; AND THEN the end will come" (Matt. 24:14; emphasis mine).*** God is giving everyone a chance to hear about Jesus and either believe or deny. (My personal opinion is that those who pass on that have never heard the gospel will be given a chance once they die and that everyone too young to make that choice or understand it will be saved by Jesus automatically and taken home to the Father for all eternity.)

Here is some tough love and hard truth, the rest of us adults need to make the most important decision there is. It is not enough for us to say that our parents didn't raise us with a belief in God. As an adult, you are responsible for seeking the answer to this question. You are responsible for investigating whether there is a God or not. Remember God wants us all to seek him. If anyone has ever told you that Jesus is your savior and you chose not to accept his free gift of salvation, you will be held accountable one day. For Jesus told us, ***"Whoever denies me before others, I will also deny to my father who is in heaven" (Matt. 10:33).*** Jesus said, ***"I am the way, the truth, and the life. No one comes to the father except through the Son" (John 14:6).*** That last part is critical. Jesus says he is the one and only ticket to heaven. This invitation is open to all! The ball is in your court. The choice is yours alone. So choose wisely because your choice will have eternal consequences. Jesus said, ***"Whoever believes and is baptized will be saved, but whoever does not believe will be condemned" (Mark 16:16).*** Jesus is the only way!

"And there is salvation in no one else, for there is no other name under heaven given among men by which we must be saved" (Acts 4:12). This is not meant to scare anybody; instead this should excite us all! This is the good news of the gospel. Jesus Christ already paid the price for your sins, and all you have to do, literally all you have to do, is accept that free gift. It truly couldn't get any easier. Eternal life is an open invitation to all of humanity. I can't stress this enough. God is so loving he allows us to decide where we will spend eternity.

We are all children of God and the rightful heirs of the kingdom of heaven. ***"And since we are his children, we are his heirs. In fact, together with Christ we are heirs of God's glory. But if we are to share in his glory, we must share his suffering" (Rom. 8:17).*** No one can take that inheritance from you. Only you can give up your salvation and chose to turn away from God. No one can steal what God has given you, but you can be dupped by the enemy and tricked into freely giving it up. Remember Jesus said, ***"The thief comes only*** *to steal, kill and destroy, I have come to give you life and have it to the full" (John 10:10).* Salvation is a God-given right and God's promise to all who accept Jesus as Lord and Savior. If you accept Jesus, you accept life; if you reject Jesus, you are alone and exposed to Satan for the taking. God's love, protection, and favor extends to all humans who seek it. Once you accept Jesus Christ, you are forever sealed to God for all eternity in the Book of Life. *"And I saw the dead, great and small, standing before the throne, and books were opened. Then another book was opened, which is the book of life. And the dead were judged by what was written in the books, according to what they had done" (Rev. 20:12).*

God already knows who will accept Jesus in the end and who will deny him. The end was written before the beginning began. God is all-knowing and all-powerful. He knows everyone who will be saved and by which means they come to salvation. We are never to write someone off as too far gone. Instead we should strive to reach those farthest from God. Only God knows the eternal destination of each of his children. You could be the key to bringing the good news of salvation to someone living in darkness. *"The one who conquers will be clothed thus in white garments, and I will NEVER blot his name out of the book of life. I will confess his name before my father and before his angels" (Rev. 3:5; emphasis mine).* When you confess that Jesus Christ is Lord and Savior, when you die, he will confess to God that you are his and that your sins have been forgiven because of his sacrifice on the cross. Those who deny Jesus will face eternal separation from God after death. *"This is the second death. Anyone not found written in the book of life was cast into the lake of fire" (Rev. 20:15).* The choice truly is yours. The good news is, if you are reading this book, you are still alive! There is still time for you to make your choice and choose Jesus and eternal life. There is also still time for you to help those around you make that choice as well.

In the end, no one can be forced to choose God, and that certainly isn't what God wants. God's gift of free will even extends to allowing you to choose your eternal destination yourself. He wants you to WANT to love him for all that he has done and created for you and all that he is. He doesn't want anyone to be forced to love him; that's not true love. Remember God knows our hearts and all our thoughts and intentions. You cannot fool God. Jesus warned we must truly know him to be saved. ***"Not everyone who says to me, 'Lord, Lord,' will enter the kingdom of heaven, but only the one who does the will of my Father who is in heaven. Many will say to me on that day, 'Lord, Lord, did we not prophesy in your name and in your name drive out demons and in your name perform many miracles?' Then I will tell them plainly, 'I never knew you, depart from me, you evildoers!'" (Matt. 7:21–23).*** You can't live a life opposing God and his goodness and then say at the last second you know Jesus and be saved. You must truly know Jesus and believe in him. ***"If you confess with your mouth that Jesus is Lord AND BELIEVE in your heart that God raised him from the dead, you will be saved" (Rom. 10:9; emphasis mine).*** This cannot be faked. Your belief must be true and wholehearted. ***"Know the God of your father and serve him with a whole heart and a willing mind: for the Lord searches all hearts and understands EVERY intent of the thoughts. If you seek him, he will let you find him; but if you forsake him, he will reject you forever" (1 Chron. 28:9; emphasis mine).***

We cannot hide anything from God. ***"Would God not find this out? For he knows the secrets of the heart" (Ps. 38:9).*** I admit this can be a scary thought. I know I have thought some pretty awful things that I'm ashamed to admit have crossed my mind. The good news is when you admit you are a sinner and you have no power to control evil in your life without Jesus, he gladly rescues us and washes us clean, removing all our transgressions. You must realize that you need a savior in order to be saved. This is the problem many face. We live in a society that tells us we are enough and we can be independent and do all things (think of all the self-help books and seminars out there); many fall for that lie. This is Satan trying to convince us that we don't need God. We must lovingly point out this flawed ideology when we see it in the world around us. The truth is none of us are enough. Only Jesus is enough, and only through accepting him as Lord over your life we ever be made enough or worthy to be in God's glorious, holy presence. Jesus must be Lord over your life to wash you clean from your sins.

"But if we walk in the light as he himself is in the light, we have fellowship with one another, and the blood of Jesus his Son cleanses us from all sin" (1 John 1:7). This is God's faithful promise and his plan to rescue humanity from eternal separation from himself. Only Jesus can stand in the gap between our sinful selves and God's holiness. Jesus is the only reason any human can stand in the presence of God. Jesus is coming back again, and when Jesus comes back again, everything will change. The second coming of Jesus will be when all believers are gathered to God forever, and all those who rejected God with be banished from his presence for all eternity. Not all of us will live through end times since no man knows when that will be, but we are all guaranteed that one day, we will all die. Our time to make this eternity-altering decision is short and unknown. You must decide where you will spend eternity now BEFORE your time runs out.

God's Remnant Takes Back the Kingdom

THE DEFINITION OF A remnant is "a small remaining quantity of something." In Christian theology, the remnant refers to the small minority of people who will remain faithful to God until the end. God speaks of the remnant of his chosen followers several times throughout the Bible. *"In that day the Lord will reach out his hand a second time to reclaim the surviving remnant of his people" (Isa. 11:11).* God is right here, right now strengthened his faithful followers and calling his church to move out and bring his love and his salvation to all that we meet. *"So too at the present time there is a remnant chosen by grace" (Rom. 11:5).* We are all chosen by the grace of God. Again, we can't earn salvation; it is a free gift from our father who loves us. It is only because of his grace and mercy that our sinful selves can be made clean and right.

There are major revivals happening all over the world right now for Christ. It is powerful to witness so many boldly speaking truth and risking their lives and reputations for the gospel. Men and women all over the planet are finding salvation in the name of Jesus. This is wonderful and amazing; however, there is still much work to be done! One look around at today's culture and it is easy to see that we are losing souls left and right to the god of this world, Satan. In 2023, a report published by the Center for the Study of Global Christianity at Gordon Conwell Theological Seminary showed that only 2.6 billion people identify as Christians. There are over eight billion people alive. The vast majority of people do not know Jesus as their savior. This is heartbreaking! Jesus said, *"I am the way, the truth and the life. No one comes to the father except through me" (James 14:6).*

It's time for true believers to get off the sidelines and get in the game and start winning souls back for God's kingdom. God says he wants none to perish but all to come to repentance. God needs all of us believers to help bring that message to those far from him before it is too late. Jesus told us he is coming back, and when he does, it will be too late. No one knows the date or the hour, but Jesus said to always be ready because it could come any time, and when it does, you can no longer sit on the fence. You are either on team Jesus or you're not, there is no in between. If you are not all in with Jesus, you will be separated from God for all eternity. This is why God so graciously has allowed us all to still be here. He wants all his precious children to enjoy eternity with him. *"The Lord is not slow in keeping his promises as some understand slowness. Instead, he is patient with you, not wanting anyone to perish, but everyone to come to repentance" (2 Pet. 3:9).*

God is giving us an unknown amount of time to bring more of our fellow man to know Jesus and be saved. These unsaved souls are our family members, our neighbors, our friends, our kids' teachers and coaches, our coworkers, and members of our local community as well as our global community. God wants us to reach people all over the world for him. God says he sends US to the ends of the earth to share the good news. In today's global society, it has never been easier to reach people all over the world. *"You will receive power when the Holy Spirit has come upon you, and you will be my witnesses in Jerusalem and in Judea and Samaria, and to all the ends of the earth" (Acts 1:8).* God is talking to us. He wants us to bring the message of Jesus Christ to all people in all places. We are to share that message and try to bring as many into the kingdom of God as we can. Jesus said, *"Come, follow me and I will make you fishers of men" (Matt. 4:19).* We are to bring as many men and women as we can to know the truth of the living God. We are to "fish for men." God will sort out the bad fish and the "keepers" at the end. It is not for us to decide who God will save, but we can be key instruments in bringing the good news of salvation to as many people as possible during our lifetime.

Time is of the essence because the amount of time we have is unknown. Jesus said, *"Therefore you must always be ready for the son of man is coming at an hour you do not expect" (Matt. 24:44).* Jesus warned us, *"The day of the Lord will come like a thief in the night" (1 Thess. 5:2).* I personally feel very strongly that the end is approaching rapidly. The warning signs are everywhere when you look at the world with spiritual eyes and with biblical insight. I feel this is the reason God was so urgently asking me to write this book. Whether it's two hundred years, fifty years, five years, or five months from now, I have no clue, and neither does any human being. The timing isn't as important as the task of preparing our souls. Jesus said there would be signs that the end is near. I personally believe many of those signs in scripture are unfolding before our very eyes. Jesus said, *"You will hear of wars and rumors of wars, but see to it that you are not alarmed. Such things must happen, but the end is still to come. Nation will rise against nation, and kingdom against kingdom. There will be famines and earthquakes in various places. All these are the beginning of birth pains" (Matt. 24:6–8).*

Jesus describes the end like birth pains. Meaning that just like contractions, the frequency and intensity will increase as we get closer to the end. We have been seeing wars and natural disasters since the beginning of time. They are, however, getting more intense, more frequent and more devasting. The date and time are not important; what is important is that the remnant, Jesus's true believers here on earth, are ready at any time and are doing everything we can to prepare not only ourselves but also those around us to be ready for whenever that time comes. We must be alert and ready to recognize the real second coming of Jesus. Jesus warns that many will come as false prophets to deceive the people of the earth, even some true believers. *"For false christs and false prophets will appear and perform great signs and wonders to deceive, if possible, even the elect" (Matt. 24:24).*

Satan is clever, and he knows what humans desire. He will use our desires against us to trick us and cause many to fall away from the one true God. Satan knows that we desire to have our own thoughts, feelings, and ideas validated. We want to feel good about the choices we make even those that are sinful. This is how he will so easily fool many with his false prophets and ideology. *"For the time is coming when people will not put up with sound doctrine. Instead, to suit their own desires, they will gather around them a great number of teachers to say what their itching ears want to hear" (2 Tim. 4:3).* We see this already in the world around us. We live in a broken society that tries to convince us that anything goes and everything is acceptable. This is a deadly trap and straight out of Satan's playbook.

God has already very clearly outlined what he expects from us and what is acceptable and righteous in his eyes and what is not. Hold tight to the truth of scripture. Guard your heart and mind with Jesus so that you will not be deceived. *"So if anyone tells you, 'There he is, out in the wilderness,' do not go out; or 'here he is, in the inner room,' do not believe it. For as lightning that's comes from the east is visible even in the west, so will be the coming of the Son of Man" (Matt. 24:26–27).* When Jesus comes back, he says it will be in the same way that he ascended to heaven after his resurrection. *"Jesus who was taken up from you into heaven, will come in the same way as you saw him go into heaven" (Acts 1:11).* He will come from the sky like lightning, and it will be visible to everyone on the face of the earth. *"Behold, he is coming with the clouds, and EVERY eye will see him" (Rev. 1:7).* When Jesus comes back, it will be obvious to all. There will be no guessing involved. This is super important so that no one is deceived. God's remnant must be aware that Satan plans to deceive even more people as the end draws closer. He will send many into the world claiming to be Jesus and the savior of the world. *"And many false prophets will arise and lead many astray" (Matt. 24:11).* But God's Word has armed us with the truth. Keep the words of scripture and the wisdom from God always at the forefront of your mind.

"My son, do not let wisdom and understanding out of your sight, preserve sound judgment and discretion; they will be life for

you, an ornament to grace your neck. Then you will go on your way in safety, and your foot will not stumble. When you lie down, you will not be afraid; when you lie down, your sleep will be sweet. Have no fear of sudden disaster or of the ruin that overtakes the wicked, for the Lord will be at your side and will keep your foot from being snared" (Prov. 3:21–26). God is saying no matter how crazy this world gets or how much evil is all around you, you have nothing to worry about if Jesus is your savior. God has got you! There is NOTHING to fear. There is nothing Satan or this world could throw at you that will take you down. Never lose sight of that truth no matter what circumstances you find yourself in. That is the wisdom from up above; God says do not let out of your sight. God is holding you up. If you are on team Jesus, you are on the winning team EVERY TIME. *"So do not fear, I am with you. Do not be dismayed, for I am your God. I will strengthen you and help you; I will uphold you with my righteous right hand" (Isa. 41:10).* Again, truth is power, and knowing the Word of God is really our only defense against the enemy's lies. God empowers his remnant to know truth through scripture and to hold steadfast to it.

Jesus already came once to save us all from our sins. His second coming will only be to gather all his faithful children to himself and bring them into heaven to be with him for all eternity. *"So Christ, having been offered once to bear the sins of many, will appear a second time, NOT to deal with sin but to save those who are eagerly waiting for him" (Heb. 9:28; emphasis mine).* Jesus promised that he was leaving to prepare a place for his followers and that he would come back to get us when God determined it was time. God will only allow sins on this earth to go unchecked for so long. God's holiness will not allow for humans to continue in their wickedness forever. Jesus will fulfill prophecy once again and come back to gather all God's loyal children to himself. Jesus promised, *"My Father's house has many rooms; if that were not so, would I have told you that I am going there to prepare a place for you? And if I go and prepare a place for you, I will come back and take you to be with me that you also may be where I am" (John 14:2–3).* If Jesus said it, rest assured it is truth. I'm sure we all have people we know and love who still have not accepted Christ. The thought of eternity without them is my motivation for this book. I want everyone I know and love to not only have the peace and joy in life of knowing Christ but also spend eternity with the one true God.

Although the Word of God may be complete in terms of the compilation of the Bible, God is not done speaking. God is eternal, and he is always at work. God is communicating with millions of believers all over the world at any given moment. The testimonies and stories of God's work in people's lives are unlimited, and each one is amazing, personal, and inspiring. God wants to give you a story of your own to share with the world that will have eternal impact. If this faith is new to you, ask for the spirit of God to guide and lead you as you navigate your new faith. Pray for godly men and women to walk alongside you and mentor you. Pray to have eyes that see only truth and ears that hear only truth. If you have already accepted Jesus as your savior, get baptized! Publicly declaring your faith and your decision to follow Jesus is a huge step in deepening your relationship with your heavenly Father.

A surrendered life to Christ is a lifelong journey, and we must choose every day to spend time with God and be in his Word in order to grow and nurture that relationship. As you begin to focus your time, energy, and resources into truly seeking the Lord, with all your heart, mind, and soul, it is then that he begins to reveal himself more fully to you. ***"Call to me and I will answer you and show you great and mighty things, which you did not know before" (Jer. 33:3).*** We are all sinners, and we are all a work in progress. It is only through the grace and mercy Jesus showed us when he died on the cross for us that is it possible for us to come before God as the broken sinners that we are. Only Jesus can fully set us free from the chains of our past failures, regrets, and sins. In doing so, we are finally able to freely step into the life God has for us. ***"If the son sets you free you are free indeed" (John 8:36).***

We don't need to have it all figured out before God can use us for his kingdom. We just must be willing to allow his will to be accomplished through our lives; he'll handle the rest. The Bible tells us, ***"God began a good work in you, and I am sure he will continue*** *it until it is finished when Jesus Christ comes again" (Phil. 1:6).* God uses every moment of our lives that we allow him to for his glory and in accomplishing his will, even our past mistakes and most definitely our pain, tears, past hurts, and traumas. *"For I know the plans I have for you declares the Lord, plans to prosper you and not to harm you, plans to give you hope and a future" (Jer. 29:11).* I know God has an incredible plan for my life and yours. God uses us, his precious children, to be his hands and feet here on earth. Jesus said, *"You are the light of the world…let your light shine before others, that they may see your good deeds and glorify your father in heaven" (Matt. 5:14, 16).*

Luckily, Jesus set me free long ago of any of my past shame and failures. This freedom I have found in Jesus is how God is able to use me today to try to help point others to truth. This book is a call to action for God's remnant here on earth. Just as Esther was encouraged of her purpose in God's kingdom by being told *"who knows but that you have come to your royal position for such a time as this" (Esther 4:14).* I also want to encourage you that the same is true for each and every one of us. We are all here together on this earth right here and now not by some cosmic accident but because it is the will of the Lord. *"From one man he made all the nations, that they should inhabit the whole earth; and he marked out their appointed times in history and the boundaries of their lands. God did this so that they would seek and perhaps reach out to him and find him, though he is not far from any one of us" (Acts 17:26–27).*

Your appointed time in history is now; do not miss out on the important role God has for you. God will strengthen you and help you along the way as you search to discover how he wants to use you for his kingdom. His plans for you are good and perfect. My hope is that you discover all that he has in store for you in this life.

Bringing It All Together

T HERE IS ONLY ONE God. He is the creator of all that is seen and unseen. God created you. He loves you, and he knows you personally and intimately. You are his precious child! Your identity comes from who God says you are, not what this world says about you. God knows you inside and out and better than you know yourself. He knows your every thought and every need. He chose you before the world began. He wants what all good fathers want, to be known and to be loved by you and to be a part of your life. Just like any human father, he wants your respect and your love. He also wants you to love and respect your fellow brothers and sisters. He wants us all to help each other out in this life. He wants us to learn how to truly love like Jesus while here on earth so that one day he will have a perfect family in heaven that loves one another. He desires a family that loves deeply and lives in perfect harmony with one another and all he has created, one that will never cause hurt or suffering again. We have all been given the same glorious gift of life on this earth. We all owe it to the same father, our Lord God in heaven.

We all have a very important mission while here on this earth to discover God, our Creator, to know him, love him, and to point and direct others to him. Our mission is to build up an eternal family that will live in perfect peace and harmony together with our Creator for all eternity once our time here on this earth is complete. God wants you to seek him and to spend time abiding in him and building a deep relationship with him. Time spent in prayer and reading scripture is how we discover who God is more fully. God reveals himself in different ways to different people at different times. The more you search for answers, the more answers he provides. God is not distant. He is always available to each of us to be fully known in a personal way. The good gifts that God has in store for those who love him are innumerable. You will never know how wonderful and full life can be until you live the life God planned for you. It is truly you who will miss out on a life well lived if you decide not to walk with Jesus in all that he calls you to do. If you rightfully prioritize your life with God at the top and his will first, he will then give you the desires of your heart as well. Your blessings will be many, and your soul will be filled with a true love and peace that only God can provide. This world can never satisfy all your needs. God didn't design it to. Only God can be your everything, and when you allow him to be, he will fill your life with goodness in ways you never even imagined.

God's existence is not dependent on your belief in him. Your existence, however, is fully dependent on God from every beat of your heart to every breath in your lungs and everything in between, whether you realize it or not. God does not force anyone to believe in him, seek a relationship with him, or choose to accept Jesus. He gives us all free will to do as we please while on this earth. This gift has huge ramifications that very few realize the eternal consequences of. Because God loves us all, as his glorious creation, he did not leave us in the dark to figure this all out for ourselves. God has revealed himself to man through his holy words in the Bible. He introduces himself to us and explains who he is and who he created us to be. God gave us his written word in scripture to show us how to live in accordance with his will. Scripture is our guide for how to live our lives, how to treat our fellow man, and how to serve God. God is the author of life. He is the beginning and the end of all that we know. God is the same yesterday, today, and tomorrow, and his promises are all true and always fulfilled.

Your belief in Jesus Christ is essential for your salvation. Salvation is a free gift that cannot be earned but is freely given to all who accept Jesus as their Lord and Savior. If you accept Jesus and allow his work on the cross to be the payment for your sins, your sins are forgiven, and you will inherit eternal life. If you chose to deny Jesus, you will have to pay for your sins yourself on the day of judgment. Every single one of us has a choice to make. This choice is the single most important decision you will ever face. Will you embrace your Creator, love him, and serve him with the time he has given you, or will you reject him? God's gift of free will puts the ball in your court. I'll reiterate because this is so important! Salvation is free, paid for by the blood of Jesus Christ. If you believe in Jesus Christ as your Lord and Savior, you are saved. By our belief in Jesus and our belief alone, we gain access to God's grace, forgiveness, and eternal life. It really couldn't get any easier.

Eternal life is yours if you want it. The choice is yours and yours alone. Choose wisely, dear friends, and God will give you the keys to the kingdom right now while you are still here on earth. He will bestow blessing upon blessing on your life and shower you with love like you've never felt before. God is patiently waiting for each of us to walk into the life he had planned for us before the world began. It's time to really use this life to be fully alive and on mission. You know the way. God has shown you through his Word and the life of Jesus. Jesus is the way.

While salvation is a free gift, a life walking with Christ will require you to serve God and serve others in love. Love is the most important thing Jesus taught us. Loving God with all your heart, mind, and soul is the key to pleasing God. God should be the number one priority in all our lives and the foundation for which we build all the other aspects of our life around. Once God is at the center and above all other things in life, only then can we naturally fulfill his second most important command: to love others as we love ourselves. God invites us all into a beautiful life filled with adventure, blessings, promises, and protection. A life walking with Christ is a life well lived. Any other path will lead to disappointment.

While God is good all the time, this world will cause us many troubles due to the presence of our great enemy, Satan and the evil forces in the unseen realm that are actively opposing God's good nature and love. God wants to teach all of us to overcome all the problems of the world by relying on him and him alone. It is imperative to think long term and know that this world and all its problems are temporary. God is in control in all things and all areas. While it feels sometimes like Satan is winning the battles, God has already won the war. Satan and all the forces of evil are under the control of our God. God has already overcome evil, and the end is written and will be fulfilled just as God promised in revelation in scripture.

We are fighting against spiritual forces of darkness on this earth; we are not fighting against our fellow brothers and sisters. All humans everywhere are victims of the same spiritual bully, Satan. We must recognize that our true enemy is not each other but the devil himself. We must all ban together and stop fighting our fellow man and start living out our true calling: to walk in the light of Christ and be God's hands and feet here on earth. We must ban together in unity to fight back against the powers of darkness. A spiritual battle is best fought in a spiritual way by prayer and rebuking the enemy at every turn with the Word of God and the truth of scripture. We can further destroy the work of our enemy with our actions by being the light of Christ to those still living in spiritual darkness around us. Martin Luther King Jr. famously said, "Darkness cannot drive out darkness: only light can do that. Hate cannot drive out hate: only love can do that." Those of us who can see God's faithfulness and know that the enemy of our souls, Satan, has no place in our lives unless we allow him access have truly overcome sin and death. We will inherit eternal life. We can bring God's kingdom here on earth by living out the example Jesus set for us. We love those who are unlovable, we forgive the unforgiveable, we bring peace to chaos and strife, we bring unity where there is division, we praise God in the storms and trials in life, and we give God all the thanks, praise, and glory in all circumstances. This is how you live as a true child of God. This is how you lead a life well lived and bring glory to your Father in heaven. This is how you have peace and fullness of life. Jesus is the way.

Friends, I want to encourage you all to never give up your faith, never stop loving and doing good to others, and never lose sight of the promises of eternal life. ***"Fight the good fight of the faith. Take hold of the eternal life to which you were called" (1 Tim. 6:12).*** May God bless and protect you all and guide you on the path to salvation. May you find the way everlasting. I pray that God will reveal your true identity to you and that you will hear from God in a very personal way as he shows you what gifts and talents he has given you to help bring his kingdom to fulfillment. May you each walk into your calling and be the light of Christ to those around you. *"I urge you to live a life worthy of the calling you have received" (Eph. 4:1).* I look forward to seeing you all in heaven one day, dear brothers and sisters.

About the Author

MICHELLE IS A WIFE, a mother, a flawed human, and a sinner. She is saved by grace and redeemed by Christ and wants to help others discover that same path to true freedom and happiness. Michelle is a part-time author and full-time lover of all things Jesus! She is passionate about the Word of God and makes it her life's mission to spread the good news of the gospel to all those who have ears to hear it.

Printed in the USA
CPSIA information can be obtained
at www.ICGtesting.com
CBHW031202050724
11009CB00003B/313